BREAKING CHAINS, BUILDING FUTURES

BREAKING CHAINS,

Pathways to Redemption, Education, and Excellence

BUILDING FUTURES

STANLEY ANDRISSE
MBA, PhD
Executive Director of Prison to Professionals
AND THIRTEEN **CO-AUTHORS**

WILEY

Copyright © 2026 by John Wiley & Sons, Inc. All rights reserved, including rights for text and data mining and training of artificial intelligence technologies or similar technologies.

Published by John Wiley & Sons, Inc., Hoboken, New Jersey.
Published simultaneously in Canada.

No part of this publication may be reproduced, stored in a retrieval system, or transmitted in any form or by any means, electronic, mechanical, photocopying, recording, scanning, or otherwise, except as permitted under Section 107 or 108 of the 1976 United States Copyright Act, without either the prior written permission of the Publisher, or authorization through payment of the appropriate per-copy fee to the Copyright Clearance Center, Inc., 222 Rosewood Drive, Danvers, MA 01923, (978) 750-8400, fax (978) 750-4470, or on the web at www.copyright.com. Requests to the Publisher for permission should be addressed to the Permissions Department, John Wiley & Sons, Inc., 111 River Street, Hoboken, NJ 07030, (201) 748-6011, fax (201) 748-6008, or online at http://www.wiley.com/go/permission.

The manufacturer's authorized representative according to the EU General Product Safety Regulation is Wiley-VCH GmbH, Boschstr. 12, 69469 Weinheim, Germany, e-mail: Product_Safety@wiley.com.

Trademarks: Wiley and the Wiley logo are trademarks or registered trademarks of John Wiley & Sons, Inc. and/or its affiliates in the United States and other countries and may not be used without written permission. All other trademarks are the property of their respective owners. John Wiley & Sons, Inc. is not associated with any product or vendor mentioned in this book.

Limit of Liability/Disclaimer of Warranty: While the publisher and author have used their best efforts in preparing this book, they make no representations or warranties with respect to the accuracy or completeness of the contents of this book and specifically disclaim any implied warranties of merchantability or fitness for a particular purpose. No warranty may be created or extended by sales representatives or written sales materials. The advice and strategies contained herein may not be suitable for your situation. You should consult with a professional where appropriate. Further, readers should be aware that websites listed in this work may have changed or disappeared between when this work was written and when it is read. Neither the publisher nor authors shall be liable for any loss of profit or any other commercial damages, including but not limited to special, incidental, consequential, or other damages.

For general information on our other products and services or for technical support, please contact our Customer Care Department within the United States at (800) 762-2974, outside the United States at (317) 572-3993 or fax (317) 572-4002.

Wiley also publishes its books in a variety of electronic formats. Some content that appears in print may not be available in electronic formats. For more information about Wiley products, visit our web site at www.wiley.com.

Library of Congress Cataloging-in-Publication Data is Available:

ISBN: 9781394321049 (paper)
ISBN: 9781394321056 (ePub)
ISBN: 9781394321063 (ePDF)

Cover Design: Paul McCarthy
Cover Art: © Getty Images | Ichiro
SKY10123370_073125

This book is dedicated to my mother, Yorvoll Joseph Andrisse. You were the matriarch and rock of our family, and even though you are no longer with us, your love and wisdom continue to guide me. Your strength and perseverance were unmatched, and I carry your spirit with me every day.

I also dedicate this book to my Haitian heritage, culture, and upbringing—everything that shaped who I am. The lessons I learned from my roots, the resilience that runs through my veins, and the love of my people have all made me who I am today. This book is a reflection of the sacrifices made and the strength cultivated in the face of adversity. Thank you for being the foundation of my journey. Peace and blessings to all who walk this path with me.

Contents

Introduction ix

PART I SYSTEMIC ISSUES 1

1 The Strength of Healed Wounds:
   From Trials to Triumph—Rewriting
   the Narrative of Justice and Purpose 3

2 Light to Life: One Mission, One Voice—A Story
   of Resilience and Advocacy 19

3 Lessons Beyond the Classroom: An Educator's
   Journey of Resilience, Redemption, and Purpose 35

4 Reentry Is Reinvention 51

PART II RESILIENCE 65

5 Resilience and Perseverance Win 67
6 Journey to Liberating the Institutionalized Mind 79
7 It Takes a Village 101
8 A House Made of Ashes 119

PART III EDUCATION AND MENTORSHIP 131

9 Fallen 133
10 The Wall: Behind and Beyond—The Evolution
    of Phillip Alvin Jones 153

11	A Stage Worthy of Freedom	169
12	The Long Road Home	187

Conclusion: Systemic Injustice, Personal
Transformation, and the Path Toward Change   *195*
Notes   *201*
Acknowledgments   *205*
About the Authors   *207*
Index   *221*

Introduction

By Dr. Stanley Andrisse

"**Ambien petit mwen, Se sa Bondye te mennen ou isit la pou fè.**"
(Well, my son. This is what God brought you here to do.)

Have you ever given deep thought to what truly drives someone's life purpose? Not the kind of purpose dictated by ambition or accolades, but the one born from struggle, love, and unyielding faith.

I didn't fully understand mine until I laid next to my mother, Yorvoll Joseph Andrisse, during one of her final days on this Earth. I was weary—physically, mentally, and emotionally—after dedicating myself to the exhausting but rewarding work of creating opportunities for the hopeless and the incarcerated. I remember breaking down into tears, questioning the toll it was taking on me, questioning why I kept going. That's when she, despite her failing body and fleeting energy, looked into my eyes with a clarity that was nothing short of divine. She simply said:

"**Ambien petit mwen, Se sa Bondye te mennen ou isit la pou fè**," which translates into, "*Well, my son. This is what God brought you here to do.*" Those words changed everything.

My mother's wisdom often came wrapped in the simplest of phrases, but they carried the weight of generations. She was a woman who, though soft-spoken in demeanor, had a strength born of hardship and a love that seemed infinite. She had known what it meant to fight—first as a Haitian immigrant navigating the challenges of a foreign land, then as a mother raising five children, and later as the matriarch of a sprawling family rooted in her values.

But her strength wasn't just for survival. It was a strength that gave. She gave her time, her care, and her essence to all who walked through our doors. Our house was not merely a home; it was a sanctuary where culture, community, and compassion lived in every plate of "diri, poul, ak pwa," which translates to rice, chicken, and beans, a celebrated bean and rice dish that gets its complex flavor profile from epis, Haiti's verdant, peppery green seasoning akin to sofrito.

We called each other "Best," not just because I was her youngest child but because we shared a bond that transcended titles. We were confidants, partners in the spirit of life, and, most importantly, believers in the good that could be done in the world.

Her legacy was built on the pillars of love, sacrifice, and purpose. She believed in doing what was right, even when it wasn't easy. It's why she and my father left the familiarity of Haiti with three young children in tow, chasing dreams of opportunity and betterment in the United States. It's why she worked tirelessly to ensure that all five of her children would go on to graduate from college. And it's why, even in her final days, she reminded me that the work I do with Prison to Professionals (P2P) isn't just a job—it's my calling.

But her guidance was never without warmth, humor, or humanity. One moment, she was a sage speaking divine truths; the next, she was frantically planning a meal of "diri, poul, ak pwa" for the "men" who would come to take her on her final journey. These were the men she said were her husband, my father, and other "soldiers," waiting to bring her home. My mother, ever the nurturer, wanted to make sure they were fed.

And so, I dedicate this book to her. To the woman whose life was a testament to resilience, faith, and unconditional love. To my mother, who saw something in me that I didn't always see in myself.

This book, *Breaking Chains, Building Futures: Pathways to Redemption, Education, and Excellence*, is about purpose—mine, hers, and that of the 13 incredible individuals whose voices fill these pages. It's about redemption, second chances, and the undeniable power of believing that, as stated in my first book's subtitle, which are the words of my father, *it is never too late to do good*. It is my honor to share these stories, grounded in authenticity and lived experience, in memory of the woman who taught me to always seek the good in others and to fight for a world where every person has the opportunity to fulfill their God-given purpose.

Rest in Paradise, Mom. Your words will forever guide me: **"Ambien petit mwen, Se sa Bondye te mennen ou isit la pou fè."** I share with you the full version of my mother's eulogy that I delivered at her funeral.

Yorvoll Andrisse's Eulogy
By Stanley Andrisse

Good morning [et Bonjour]. I'm Stanley Andrisse, the youngest of Yorvoll Andrisse's five children. Thank you for attending this ceremony honoring the beautiful life of my mother. Yorvoll Joseph Andrisse was not simply my mother. She was my best friend. She was the rock of our family.

Mon héritage haïtien et la patrie haïtienne de ma famille. A fait de moi qui je suis.

Eritaj ayisyen mwen an ak peyi ayisyen fanmi an. Li fè mwen moun mwen ye.

That was in French and Kreyol. Which translates to, "My Haitian heritage and culture. My family's Haitian homeland and my Haitian cultural upbringings have made me who I am."

In essence, what I just said was … we grew up on "diri, poul, ak pwa" … "rice, chicken, and beans." "Diri, poul, ak pwa" was what was for dinner *five* out of the seven days of the week. To the non-Haitians in the audience that may sound boring. But there are 101 different ways to make "diri, poul, ak pwa." There's "sòs pwa blan," "sòs pwa wouj," "sòs pwa nwa," "poul ak epis," "poul ak piman."

It was anything but boring. On the contrary, several of my siblings have asked my mom to teach their significant others to make "diri, poul, ak pwa." Growing up, our house was the neighborhood gathering place for eating delicious food that was different. My siblings' and [my] friends would readily be at the dinner table, and my mom would serve them as her own children. Some of them, possibly sucking up to get more "griot et banan peze," called her "Best," as I did.

My mom and I called each other "Best" because when I was very little, I repeatedly told her that she would be my best friend forever. Even when I went off and got married, she would still be my best friend. And to her last breath, we continued to call each other Best, and she remains my best friend.

This day is a profoundly sad one. In this time of grief, I encourage us to reflect on the many wonderful experiences that we shared with my mom. As you interact with each other today and in the days to come, share your most meaningful memories of Yorvoll with someone.

It's important that we acknowledge and *fully* experience the emotions of this day, on which we have gathered together to say goodbye to my mom. It is imperative to sit in the human experience of grief.

To my mom, family always came first. Being a mom to five children, a grandmother to 14 grandchildren, and a wife to my father were a few of things my mom cherished most in life. In August 2010, my dad, William Andrisse, passed away just days after celebrating 43 years of marriage with my mom. This year would have marked 55 years of marriage.

My mother and father's coming to the United States is deserving of its very own book. As such, devoting a few words cannot begin to do it justice. My mother and father met as teenagers and were married by age 22 in August 1967. My dad was one of the youngest of 10 siblings. My mom had one biological brother and several half siblings. My mom's mom, Odette, died when my mother was a toddler. My daughter's middle name is Odette after her great grandmother. Through my daughter, my mom got an additional four years with Odette. By their mid-twenties while still in Haiti, my parents had my two oldest sisters, Sherer and Yorvoll, and soon-after, my oldest brother, Vladimir. In 1980, with three kids—a six-, nine-, and ten-year-old—my parents left Haiti and came to the United States, where I and my closest brother, William, were born. Due to challenges associated with being foreigners, my family bounced around from Miami to New York to Detroit to eventually landing here in St. Louis.

For 42 years, my mom grew roots here in St. Louis. Mom to five college graduates. Grandmother to over a dozen grandkids, several of which are college graduates, most recently Alanna Marie Andrisse just this past Friday. Friend to many in the local and national Haitian community. A lover of life and all things family. Her youngest grandchild, my son, Ti William, is named after her husband, my

Introduction

father. She was able to spend a year with Baby William before joining her Husband William. From the hands of God, the greatest author of all time, my mom has a picture with Baby William, just weeks ago, where he is wearing a cute little hat that says "My first Thanksgiving." This past Thanksgiving was my mom's last Thanksgiving and the last holiday with our family.

My mom was a strong woman. When my dad passed, 12 years ago, we were unsure how she would handle his loss. But moving deeper into her role as matriarch of this family, she guided us with love and grace. My mom was a joyful and fun-loving spirit. We have many videos of her dancing with kids and grandkids to the likes of Rihanna and Drake, and her singing along, "Oh Nan Nan, What's Name." My mom embodied keeping it real and telling you how she felt. She'd hit you with the Haitian, "Umpf," and follow with, "Ambien petit mwen. Keetay mwen di ou on bagay," "Well, son. Let me tell you something."

To end, I leave you with one of the final stories of my mom. To add context to this story, in my mom's last days, she lost her hearing, sight, and did not talk very clearly. But on this day, she could see my shirt and face, she could hear me without me repeating myself, and she spoke more clearly than I'd heard in about two-years. A few weeks ago, I was visiting my mom after a long four days of being one of the organizers of a conference called STEM-OPS, which stands for Science, Technology, Engineering, and Math Opportunities in Prison Settings. We help people who are deemed hopeless find hope and opportunity. It's absolutely exhausting work. I was tired and beat down. I laid next to my mom, hugged her, and broke down into tears, asking,

"Why am I exhausting myself like this?." She said to me, very clearly, lovingly looking me in the eyes, **"Ambien petit mwen, Se sa Bondye te mennen ou isit la pou fè."** Which translates as, "Well, my son. This is what God brought you here to do."

A few minutes of silence went by, then she again very clearly asked me, "Are those men still in the room?" I said, "Mom, Se nou sèlman nan chanm lan." "It's only us in the room." She then frantically proceeded to tell me a grocery list of food items to go buy from the store. I entertained the conversation since she was so adamant. She finally told me who the men were. It was Papou, my dad, and several military men. She said they'd be back soon to get her and she wanted to prepare them some "diri, poul, ak pwa" for their journey.

My mom was ready. My dad was ready for her too. I pray that we, here, be ready. From all of us, we love you, Best. Rest in Paradise.

That was my mother's eulogy. Thank you for taking the time to absorb some of her light. A light that she has bequeathed to me. A light that I now pass along to you and the world. I have yet to share with you the most profound part of this story, "Ambien petit mwen, Se sa Bondye te mennen ou isit la pou fè." My mom did not like P2P. Or better phrased, my mom was weary or scared of P2P. My mom adamantly wanted me to put prison in the past and lock it away, never to be seen or discussed ever again.

The Unspoken Legacy: A Mother's Love and the Weight of Incarceration

I've always wondered about the weight of silence—the heavy silence that surrounds incarceration, particularly in Black families. It's a silence steeped in shame, in fear, in a deep, aching desire to protect loved ones from the harsh truths of a system that has been designed to fail them. Michelle Alexander's *The New Jim Crow* explores the way that mass incarceration functions as a system of racial control, but in the quiet corners of Black homes, it manifests in a more intimate way—through the unspoken tension, the whispered conversations, and the quiet plea to forget, to bury it all deep. My mother was no different.

Growing up in the Ferguson-Florissant area of North St. Louis County and being raised in an immigrant family from Haiti, there was an unspoken rule in my house: you did not talk about the past. You did not speak about prison. You did not speak about my mistakes. You didn't speak about what the system had done to us, to me. To talk about it was to acknowledge its power over us, to give it control over our narrative. My mother, as much as she loved me, wanted to shield me from the ugly truths. She wanted to protect me from the pain of being labeled by society, from the brutal reality that once you enter those prison gates, the world has a way of branding you, never allowing you to be seen as anything other than what the system says you are. And in that desire to protect me, she also wanted to erase it—to sweep it under the rug like it never happened.

She once told me that she cried … every single night … that I was incarcerated. I remember her saying, time and again, "Don't go back. Don't look back. You're not that person anymore." She believed it. She wanted so badly for it to be true. But the reality of it was much more complex. As the child of a Haitian immigrant family, as a young Black man from St. Louis seemingly destined to be caught in the systemic web of incarceration, I wasn't afforded the luxury of erasure. My history, my pain, my past, all of it—whether I spoke it aloud or not—was written on my skin.

In many ways, my mom's voice echoed the feelings of so many other Black mothers, especially in a community where incarceration is not a rarity but a common thread that binds us. Our families often become prisoners of this silence. No one wants to speak of it. No one wants to admit that the police, the courts, and the prison industrial complex have broken their children. They don't want the world to know. They don't want to be judged. The truth is that many of us, the families of the incarcerated, are burdened by shame. We are ashamed that our loved ones have been locked away, forgotten by the world, reduced to a number. We're ashamed that the very system meant to protect us is often the one that traps us, forces us into a cycle we can never escape.

But I was always my mother's best friend, even in the face of this silence. Even when on her death bed she told me, "Ambien petit mwen, Se sa Bondye te mennen ou isit la pou fè," she did so with love, with fear, and with a prayer that maybe, just maybe, my story could be different. She had through divine intervention come to a new understanding where she didn't want me to live in the shadow of prison. She wanted me to step into the light, to rise above it. She said, "That is what God brought me here to do" ... to find something better, something beyond the confines of a system that had always sought to control us. Yet, in her weariness and fear, in her refusal to speak of the pain, I could feel her love. She wanted me to be free, in every sense of the word. But freedom is not something you can escape simply by pretending the chains aren't there.

When I founded the organization P2P, my mother was hesitant. She didn't understand it. She didn't see the possibility in it the way I did. She didn't grasp that I was standing in the forefront of a movement. A new way of seeing *us*. To her, it felt like stepping into the past, like revisiting the trauma that we had so carefully hidden away. She wanted to protect me from that. She feared that engaging with P2P, with people who had been where I had been, would somehow undo the progress I had made, and would drag me back into a past I had fought so hard to escape. It was an understandable fear. She didn't want to risk my future by revisiting the very thing that had broken me. But what she was slow to see was that P2P wasn't about the past—it was about the future, about healing, about reclaiming that which the system had stolen from us.

Yet, there is power in facing the past. There is power in owning your story. I came to understand that the only way to fully escape the grip of the system is to break the silence, to speak about it, to tell the world what it means to be both a man and a product of that system. P2P gave me the opportunity to reclaim my narrative, to rewrite it. It gave me a way to heal and, in doing so, to help others heal as well.

In my mother's eulogy, I spoke of the light she had given me—the light that had guided me through the darkest times. That light was not just love; it was strength, it was resilience, it was the unwavering belief that no matter the scars, no matter the chains, I was still capable of something greater. It is a light that I now pass on to others, to those still trapped in the prison industrial complex, to the families who feel they have lost their loved ones to a system that profits off of their pain. That light is the possibility of redemption, of second chances, and of the chance to tell our stories on our own terms.

The work of P2P is not just about helping those who have been incarcerated—it's about breaking the silence, about telling the truth, about confronting the system that seeks to erase us. And that is where the stories in this book begin. The authors, like so many others, faced a system that tried to define them by their past. But they refused to let that system hold them forever. And through P2P, they began the hard, transformative work of reclaiming their future. These are their stories. And in telling it, we begin the work of telling our collective story—one that is not just about surviving but about thriving, not just about surviving the prison industrial complex, but about dismantling it, brick by brick.

We Demand a Seat at the Table

We demand a seat at the table. The leadership table. The funding table. The NIH study section table. The high-impact authorship table. All are places we deserve to be, yet you don't find faces like mine in places like these. You certainly don't find experiences like mine.

I am a formerly incarcerated person with three felony convictions, sentenced to 10 years in prison as a prior and persistent career criminal. I was told by a prosecutor that I had no hope for change. I am now Dr. Stanley Andrisse, endocrine scientist and assistant professor at Howard University College of Medicine, former faculty at Johns Hopkins Medicine, and former visiting faculty at Imperial College of London and Georgetown University Medical Center. Learn more about my journey to science in my first book, a "#1 New Release in Educator Biographies on Amazon (in 2021)," titled *From Prison Cells to PhD: It is Never Too Late to Do Good.*

During my incarceration, my father's type 2 diabetes worsened, and he eventually lost his battle with the disease. Dealing with this emotional pain while being locked in a cage was indescribably difficult. But I turned that pain into purpose and began studying diabetes and the intricacies of the human cell while in my prison cell.

For those who have never experienced reading a scientific article, every other word is something that you have never heard of. And there is no Google, WebMD, or ChatGPT in prison. It took months to read every article. But although my body was physically locked in a prison cell, my mind was freely roaming the human cell, floating through the cytoplasm, traveling the maze of the mitochondrial structures, and landing on DNA double helices in the nucleus. And in that way I was free. I had freed my mind from incarceration, long before my body was freed from incarceration.

The general public has a 1 in 3 chance of attaining a college degree. Due to a number of barriers and collateral consequences of incarceration like the ones I faced,[1] such as the criminal conviction question on applications, the stigma and perception of incarceration, the barriers to housing and financial aid, and the mental health issues resulting from the traumas of incarceration, a formerly incarcerated person's chances of obtaining higher education are less than 1 in 20.[2]

Societal Barriers: The Problem Is Embedded in Our Institutions

Systemic inequality has led to racial, economic, and educational disparities that are deeply entrenched in all U.S. institutions, including universities, scientific journals, and funding entities. Historically, Black and brown individuals have been excluded from the resources and funding table. I serve on the NIH Working Group on Diversity,[3] which helped produce data showing that despite Black and brown individuals making up more than 30% of the population, they received only 6% of big money NIH grants.[4] I have had the opportunity to serve on two NIH study sections, MCE-2020 and CHHDR-2021, both of which I was the only Black person on the committee. NIH data showed that only 2% of study section members are Black.[5] Now imagine how few formerly incarcerated people are likely in these groups.

Why does that matter? "The diverse group almost always outperforms the group of the best by a substantial margin," wrote Scott E. Page, social scientist and distinguished university professor. NIH is interested in the benefits of a diverse workforce on scientific discovery, and thus should include currently and formerly incarcerated people (CIP and FIP) under the NIH definition of disadvantaged groups.[6] Quality of life metrics are all significantly below average for CIP and FIP.[7] We are a disadvantaged group.

Society Is Missing Out on Talent

The nonprofit I co-founded, From Prison Cells to PhD (P2P),[8] helps CIP and FIP obtain college and STEM education. Additionally, P2P consults with employers and universities, such as Johns Hopkins and Imperial College of London, to improve their hiring and admissions strategies around equity, diversity, and inclusion. Learn more about P2P's training program at https://www.fromprisoncellstophd.org/consulting--training.html.

Higher education reduces recidivism, where 65–70% of people that step out of prison step back within five years of release; obtaining higher education reduced recidivism by 43%.[9] Nearly 30% of the general public has a college degree, compared to less than 4% of formerly incarcerated people.[10] That is a nearly ninefold difference. Science and academia need to open the door and create specific fellowships, opportunities, and funding for this disadvantaged group. Society will benefit from having CIP and FIP at the table.

Key Drivers of Incarceration

Have you ever given deep thought into why people go to prison?

It's easy to reduce incarceration to individual choices or personal failings, but the truth is far more intricate and unsettling. Behind every statistic lies a web of systemic issues—economic, racial, and societal—that pull individuals into the criminal justice system. These aren't abstract concepts; they are forces that shape lives and communities every single day. Let's explore some of the key drivers that create this reality.

Poverty

Imagine a life where every decision is a calculation of survival. Poverty isn't just about low income; it's about limited choices. Studies show that people living in poverty are significantly more likely to engage in illegal activities—not because they want to but because they must.[11] According to a report by the Prison Policy Initiative, 60% of people in jail have incomes below the poverty line. When economic hardship leaves people with few alternatives, the justice system often becomes their trap rather than their savior.

Racial and Ethnic Disparities

What happens when the system sees you differently because of the color of your skin?

Black, Latino, and Indigenous individuals are incarcerated at alarmingly disproportionate rates due to structural racism embedded in policing, sentencing, and prison systems.[12] Black Americans, for example, make up only 13% of the U.S. population but represent 40% of the prison population (NAACP). These disparities aren't just numbers—they reflect lives disrupted, families torn apart, and generations set back.

The War on Drugs

Think back to the 1980s and 1990s—did you notice the dramatic escalation of harsh drug policies? The "War on Drugs" turned what should have been a public health issue into a criminal one.[13] Mandatory minimum sentences for nonviolent drug offenses disproportionately targeted marginalized communities, filling prisons with people who needed treatment, not incarceration. Today, the remnants of these policies still contribute to mass incarceration.

Mental Health and Substance Abuse

Have you ever considered how we, as a society, treat people with mental illness or addiction?

Often, the answer is incarceration. Nearly 37% of people in prison have been diagnosed with a mental health disorder, and many struggle with substance abuse (Bureau of Justice Statistics). Without adequate care or support, they're criminalized instead of rehabilitated.[14] Prisons have become the de facto mental health institutions in the United States, a role they are ill-equipped to fill.

Harsh Sentencing Policies

Mandatory minimums. Three-strikes laws. Truth-in-sentencing policies. These laws don't just punish—they destroy futures. Harsh sentencing policies have led to a dramatic increase in the length of prison stays, often for nonviolent offenses. According to The Sentencing Project,[15] people in prison today serve sentences 20% longer on average than they did in 2000. Is justice served by excessive punishment, or is it undermined?

Over-Policing in Certain Communities

What happens when your neighborhood feels like a war zone? For many low-income and minority communities, over-policing is a daily reality. Increased police presence doesn't mean increased safety—it means higher arrest rates and a pipeline to prison. The Brookings Institution reports that Black Americans are 3.6 times more likely to be arrested than their white counterparts for the same offenses.[16]

Criminalization of Poverty

Imagine being jailed for being poor. That's not hyperbole—it's reality for many. People are incarcerated because they can't pay fines, post bail, or avoid penalties associated with homelessness.[17] In 2018, the U.S. Commission on Civil Rights found that wealth-based detention is a significant driver of incarceration, particularly for pretrial detainees.

Education Inequity

What happens when education fails an entire community?

Access to quality education is one of the strongest predictors of incarceration. High dropout rates and poorly funded schools in marginalized areas create a cradle-to-prison pipeline.[18] A report by the National Education Association highlights that a student who doesn't graduate high school is 63 times more likely to be incarcerated than one who earns a four-year college degree.

Privatization of Prisons

What if incarceration isn't about justice but profit? The rise of for-profit prisons has introduced a dangerous incentive: more people in prison equals more money. According to the Sentencing Project,[19] private prisons house 8% of the prison population but exert significant influence over policies that promote incarceration.

Lack of Rehabilitation Programs

When someone finishes their sentence, what's next? Without effective job training, education, or reentry programs, many formerly incarcerated individuals face a revolving door back to prison.[20] According to the Bureau of Justice Statistics, 68% of released prisoners are rearrested within three years. Rehabilitation isn't a luxury—it's a necessity.

Have you ever thought about what people should, could, or deserve to do when they return home?

This book explores those questions with profound detail and authenticity. Through the voices of 13 individuals who participated in the Prison to Professionals (P2P) program, we'll dive into stories of redemption, reinvention, and resilience. These are not just tales of survival—they are blueprints for transformation.

Dr. Stan Andrisse and his siblings celebrating their mom's 70th birthday, January 2014

Dr. Stan Andrisse and his mom on her 70th birthday, January 2014

Introduction

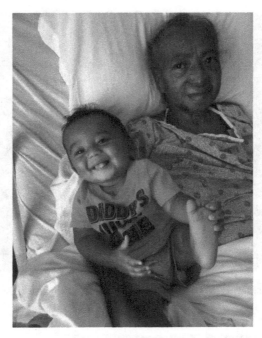

Dr. Andrisse's son, William, and his grandmother Yorvoll, two weeks before her passing, c. Thanksgiving 2022

Celebrating the beautiful life of Yorvoll Andrisse (older pic)

Part I
Systemic Issues

Chapter 1

The Strength of Healed Wounds: From Trials to Triumph—Rewriting the Narrative of Justice and Purpose

By Oswald Newbold II

Introduction to Oswald Newbold II's Chapter

By Stanley Andrisse

When I first met Oswald Newbold II, I was struck by his remarkable blend of resilience and professionalism. A man who once navigated the maze of the criminal justice system, Oswald has since become a beacon of transformation and leadership in the reentry field. His story is one of triumph over systemic barriers, driven by his unwavering commitment to uplift others through his work and advocacy.

Oswald's journey sheds light on some of the most pressing drivers of incarceration in our society—poverty, racial disparities, and harsh sentencing policies. These systemic issues not only shaped his path but also fueled his determination to break cycles of injustice and inequality. With more than 32 years of expertise spanning personal lived experience and professional practice, he exemplifies how knowledge and lived wisdom can be a powerful force for change.

(continued)

> *(continued)*
>
> Through P2P, I have witnessed Oswald grow sharper in his professional endeavors while embracing the value of his personal story to inspire others. He has courageously leaned into his worth, transforming not only his own life but also the lives of those he mentors and supports. This chapter delves into Oswald's experiences, the lessons he has garnered, and the profound impact of his work on reentry and beyond.
>
> Oswald's narrative serves as a testament to the boundless potential that lies within all of us to rebuild, redefine, and reclaim our futures. It is an honor to share his story with the world.

In first grade, I was attending a predominantly Black elementary school, Lincoln Elementary, unaware that racial prejudice was already undermining my educational dreams. Desperate to hide failing grades I received from a prejudiced teacher, I altered my report card as good as a six-year-old child could, while at the same time, unknowingly sparking a lifelong fight against systemic injustice. This traumatic experience shattered my innocence and forever changed my view concerning education and my role within learning environments. This chapter explores how early experiences of racial prejudice and educational injustice ignited my lifelong commitment to combating systemic inequalities, transforming personal struggles into a dedicated advocacy for criminal justice reform and hope within my community.

Raised in Riviera Beach's Stonybrook Apartments, near West Palm Beach, I encountered the hardships of life early on. Born to teenage parents during the economic downturn of the 1970s and surrounded by racial prejudice, my upbringing was a daily battle against systemic injustices. Stonybrook, a product of the Housing and Urban

Development Act of 1968, was meant to aid low-income families through housing and rental subsidies. Research later revealed that individuals raised in public housing are twice as likely to be incarcerated (Farrington & Welsh, 2007). Despite never envisioning myself as part of these statistics, I found myself incarcerated. Through faith, motivation, mentorship, and education, I achieved an unimaginable comeback.

To understand my journey, we must revisit the early injustice when I was six. After receiving my first-grade report card filled with Ns for "Needs Improvement" and Us for "Unsatisfactory," panic set in. Knowing the disappointment it would bring, I chose to alter the grades before showing them to my mother.

Quickly, I used the typewriter my grandmother had given me, along with some Wite-Out, to change the bad grades on my report card. With a short time before my mother's return from work, I couldn't fix every grade. The rushed modifications containing crooked letters and blobs of Wite-Out seemed sufficient to my six-year-old eyes.

When my mother got home, I gave her the altered masterpiece. Instantly, my mother noticed something was wrong and asked why the report card looked messy. I said the teacher gave it to me that way. Next, she asked about the Ns and Us I received as grades. I said I didn't know how I got those grades. Suspicious, my mother let it go. Or so I thought, until I felt a belt hitting across my back. All I can remember is crying and insisting I didn't know how I got the bad grades.

My mother found my old school papers, revealing consistently good grades, contradicting my recent poor report card. After failed phone calls to set up a parent–teacher conference, she went to the school, showing the principal my work and altered report card. The teacher, who was white, was unable to verify any failing grades inside her grade book. Yet, she was rude to my mother in front of the principal.

After the conference, the principal, who was also white, explained that the teacher was problematic and moved me to another class. On the way home, I asked my mother what had happened. She replied that the teacher was prejudiced. Not understanding the term, I asked what it meant, and in frustration, my mother blurted, "The teacher doesn't like you because of the color of your skin" (C. Hayes, personal communication, 1978). This left me confused about how my skin color could affect my grades, and I began to withdraw from striving for academic success.

Looking back, I'm grateful my mother challenged the teacher's unfair grading. But I wonder how many other students suffered because their parents trusted the grades without question. I doubt I was the only one affected. Some parents may have punished their children unjustly, not realizing the real failure was the school system.

By fourth grade, the damage was already done. I was skipping class and avoiding attention, doing just enough to stay out of trouble. My love for sports kept me maintaining fair grades. In fifth grade, I was placed in my grandmother's class but was sent to another teacher, who sent me back, saying I wouldn't pay attention. My grandmother forced me to tighten up. In sixth grade, I improved as a student safety patrol and earned a trip to Washington, DC, but afterward, I started slacking again. By then, I was ready for junior high and didn't care much about elementary school. My disengagement from education was deeply rooted in subconscious ways I didn't understand at the time.

In seventh grade, I experienced solid academic and social growth, but it was in eighth grade that I began to see education positively. I was at John F. Kennedy Junior High. I no longer lived in Stonybrook, but it remained a powerful symbol of "The Struggle" and the desire for a better life.

As a youngster, I didn't realize how much peers influence whether we strive to excel or slack off. In junior high, I met students in advanced and honors classes who were smart and cool—challenging the stereotype of intelligence as "nerdy." They looked like me, inspiring me to join their ranks. I changed my schedule on my own to get into advanced and honors classes. Though classes like algebra were challenging due to missing foundational knowledge like pre-algebra, I worked hard, studied, and asked questions. Academically, I improved. Socially, I expanded, and I began dreaming of high achievement in high school. But the dream was short-lived.

In ninth grade at North Shore HS, I reconnected with old friends and switched from advanced to regular classes, telling my counselor, "I just want to be normal." Dropping out of those classes was a mistake. By the end of the year, I was skipping classes again. It was also in ninth grade that I met my two lifelong best friends. One of them, Edwin, skipped classes more than I did, and by tenth grade, we were skipping school entirely. We knew about every high school in the county, except the one we were supposed to attend.

Around this time, home life became difficult, and at the age of 15 I ran away from home, moving to Tampa, Florida, to live with friends. It was in Tampa I started selling crack. I had no ambition, dreams, or direction.

A year later, I returned to Palm Beach County and attended Palm Beach Gardens HS for eleventh grade. The school had a small Black student population and wasn't welcoming to Black students or parents. Despite my mother's objections, I attended because I was living with my paternal grandmother in the district. After just a week and a half, I transferred following an incident where my science teacher blatantly discriminated against Black students by withholding class information she had just given to white students. Her behavior, accepted as normal at the school, deepened my disconnection from education.

The School District of Palm Beach County has a reputation as one of Florida's most racially problematic districts, due to disparities in discipline, academic achievement, racial incidents, and legal actions. Black students are 4.2 times more likely, and Hispanic students 1.4 times more likely, to be suspended than their white peers (ProPublica, n.d.). There are significant achievement gaps, with Black and Hispanic students often underperforming compared to white students (Steinhardt, NYU, 2016). Advocacy groups and the U.S. Department of Education have criticized the district for not addressing these disparities, leading to a federal investigation in 2025 (JNS, 2025).

Ironically, there I was four decades earlier dealing with the same discriminatory issues the school district is still struggling with today. It's safe to say, in less than two weeks, I left Palm Beach Gardens HS. I transferred to Suncoast HS in Riviera Beach, the alma mater of my father and mother. My mother told me I got everything I deserved for going to Palm Beach Gardens, because she told me not to go there in the first place.

At Suncoast, during the third week of my eleventh-grade year, a conversation with an old classmate who balanced school by day and hustling by night changed my outlook. I had considered dropping out but, motivated by his determination to graduate, I decided to at least try. I attended night school and summer school to catch up and became more focused when the school became a magnet school in my twelfth-grade year.

Despite academic progress, I was persuaded by an Army recruiter to join the U.S. Army for structure and discipline. I enrolled in the delayed entry program, set to leave for basic training after graduation. However, my grandfather, a Korean War veteran, and my two best friends in the Navy convinced me to reconsider. One, who left the Navy with an honorable discharge, talked me out of it. The recruiter was upset, but I didn't care. I graduated on time, scored well on the ACT, and was accepted to Florida A&M University.

College offered me a fresh start. As a freshman, I lived on campus in Gibbs Hall and played in the World Famous FAMU Marching 100.

While I marched, Operation Desert Storm unfolded in Kuwait, and I missed the war. Despite the opportunity, I took college for granted, bringing unresolved pain and negative behavior. Later, I realized my actions stemmed from trauma, but at the time, I was unaware of it.

Though I haven't talked much about my family, my family has always been a big part of my life, and I love them. It would take a tough time for me to realize how much my family loves me. My mother, father, brother, grandparents, uncles, aunts, cousins, godparents, and best friends (who are like family) have all inspired me to keep pushing forward. Life is full of highs and lows, and sometimes we're in the valley, thinking we're on a hill.

At FAMU, I experienced troubled relationships. My girlfriend from home got pregnant before I left, but her parents forced an abortion, and we didn't speak again for 20 years. I later dated someone at school, but after we broke up, she got pregnant by someone else, making me think maybe I had been the "side dude." Distrustful, I decided to have fun instead. But then I started dating someone very different from me—loud and outgoing, while I was quiet and serious. Though I was both a great and terrible boyfriend, she planted good seeds in me. Unfortunately, it took years for those seeds to grow, and only after legal troubles did I finally listen, but by then, it was too late.

I majored in criminal justice and minored in political science, developing a deep respect for Dr. Owusu Ansah Agyapong, chair of the School of Sociology and Criminal Justice, who was also my professor. He introduced our class to sentencing disparities and the significant impact of race and socioeconomic class. My own experiences with race in school made me deeply connect with his work, and while considering law, Dr. Agyapong sparked my passion for justice.

I began enjoying college but lacked discipline in my study habits. During marching band season, I performed better with limited time for homework, but in the off-season, I procrastinated and missed assignments. My academic discipline worsened after I was suspended from the band. This turbulent period, filled with distrust, hurt, and anger, contributed to the development of a bitter and hostile attitude within me.

Feeling overwhelmed as my life spiraled, one day I went to Dr. Agyapong's office to talk but left after becoming impatient with the wait. Later, he saw my name on the news and realized I had been reaching out earlier that day. He had hoped I would return, but I never did, and the realization devastated him.

At 19 years old, during my sophomore year, my attitude led to six charges across two cases. A year later, I was convicted on three charges: burglary, attempted murder, and aggravated battery. Despite Dr. Agyapong speaking on my behalf, I was sentenced to two life terms plus 15 years. At barely 20 years old, I felt sorrow, remorse, embarrassment, and shame for the harm I caused. Anger and hurt followed, but I vowed never to return to the dark place that led me here. The shame I brought upon my family made me feel low.

I was anxious about entering prison, and my arrival at North Florida Reception Center, once one of Florida's worst prisons, only heightened that anxiety. Though I had a tough attitude, I quickly realized how much power the guards abused. To survive, I had to swallow my pride, knowing resistance could mean never getting out. In my first year, my two life sentences were reduced to a 40-year and 15-year sentence, served consecutively for a total of 55 years. Education wasn't on my mind, and after five months, I was placed in solitary confinement for a drug deal gone wrong, leading to robbery and assault. This was the first of several stints in confinement.

For years, I focused on studying law in the prison law library to challenge my 55-year sentence. My sentencing guideline allowed for a range of 12 to 27 years, but the court aggravated my sentence using the same factors to both score and increase the sentence, which is impermissible in law. I realized that the flaws in legal application stemmed not only from the law itself, but more so, from biased judges and underperforming lawyers. As I studied, I began preparing my own motions, uncovering inconsistencies in the system and injustices from unequal legal treatment, which violates the 14th Amendment's promise of equal treatment under the law.

A 2017 report by the United States Sentencing Commission found that Black male offenders received sentences that were, on average, 19.1% longer than those of white male offenders for similar crimes, even after accounting for various sentencing factors (United States Sentencing Commission, 2017).

Over the years, I represented myself in cases from state courts to the U.S. Supreme Court. Through studying court rules, researching case law, and preparing pleadings, I gained valuable insight into the legal process. While I lost more cases than I won, these experiences revealed the flaws in the American justice system and fueled my advocacy for policy change. In addition, I invested in the future by engaging with students in criminal justice and related fields to influence real change.

While in a North Florida facility, my mentor, Dr. Agyapong, visited and shared how my situation changed his approach with students, highlighting the importance of addressing students in crisis. He encouraged me to stay in criminal justice, offering hope for opportunities in reform and advocacy. His influence shapes my work today on issues like racial bias in law enforcement approaches, sentencing disparities, the school-to-prison pipeline, post-incarceration reintegration, and voting rights restoration for justice-impacted individuals.

Initially, I refused classes, believing education couldn't help with my long sentences. For the first 15 years, I focused on studying law and serving my time. I can't say I was a model prisoner, because I took occasional trips to confinement.

Throughout the years, my family supported me: my parents, Cassandra and Oswald Sr.; my grandparents, Felix, Rosa, Ella, and Catherine; my brother Kevin and sister-in-law Kenya; my close friends Edwin, Desmond, and Robert Jr.; and many uncles, aunts, and cousins. I honor them, including those who passed before I was free, by doing my best daily. After God, my family and friends kept me hopeful for better days. Sadly, Dr. Agypong passed away before I could make it home.

In 2006, when my last grandparent passed, I had a revelation: I needed to do something for myself. My friend Edwin encouraged me to take advantage of the free schooling available at the facility, and a mentor pointed out that I needed a skill or trade. An old college schoolmate also encouraged me to enroll, but I kept lying about being on the waiting list for computer class. One day, after another call, I realized I was just avoiding school. Determined to change, I told the education director I wanted to enroll in a business computer software class. She put me in a night class immediately. It turned out to be one of the best decisions I made.

Taking the time to master computer skills was one of my best decisions, as it's hard to function without them. The course quickly showed me how outdated my skills were. Despite thinking of myself as smart, I felt lost in class, not even knowing what a cursor was. After 15 years in prison, I realized I needed to catch up on education and skills. The 10-month computer course turned into a three-year journey due to breaks between teachers, but each time, I relearned faster and got closer to mastering the computer.

Thank goodness for mentorship: people who were positive voices in my life and helped me find direction. This includes my fellow brothers locked up with me behind the fences, as well as those on the outside who kept me motivated and believed in me. Reflecting on my youth, I thought about the people who paid attention in school and how their lives turned out. It inspired me to apply myself to learning. For the remainder of my sentence—another 10 years—I consistently committed to self-improvement.

As I mentioned in *The Joseph Anointing: From Prison to Prosperity*: "In the last 10 years in the pit, I didn't view myself as a prisoner. I saw myself as a student and teacher. I took vocational trades, participated in self-betterment programs, engaged in independent study, created business plans with action steps, and took training. I led and facilitated life skills classes, leadership classes, disease awareness classes, and therapeutic community programs. I strengthened communication with family and friends, built a strong rapport, and shared my ideas to get feedback. Six years before my release, my reentry plan was already created. Over the years, the plan didn't change—it just got fine-tuned" (McCray, 2022, p. 27).

Over time, I realized that society's workforce relies on degrees, licenses, and certifications, and I needed to figure out how to survive post-incarceration. I saw many men return to prison, but I was determined not to be one of them. A conversation with a doctor about her overwhelming student loan debt solidified my decision to avoid school if it meant taking on debt. I vowed to pursue higher education only if it was funded by a scholarship or other means.

Finding my purpose wasn't a solo journey. I realized I was solution-oriented and enjoyed connecting meaningfully with others and organizing systems, but it took others to help me recognize my strengths in working with people and resolving conflict. Over time, I began to believe in myself.

Everything I did was preparing me to go home. When I told my family I needed clothes because I was coming home, they thought I was joking. They didn't know the Department of Corrections had restored 330 days of gain-time I'd lost for disciplinary reasons. After years of waiting, when they realized it was real, excitement filled the air. On January 17, 2017, after serving 25 years, 1 month, and 13 days, I was free.

Upon release, I carried four state licenses for restricted-use pesticides, earned through training with the University of Florida's Institute of Food and Agricultural Sciences. I also completed conflict mediation training approved by the Florida Supreme Court, which would later prove valuable in my career. Additionally, I passed the written test for a Class-A commercial driver's license and, after release, enrolled in trucking school to earn my license.

After I was released, reality hit. No amount of preparation can fully equip someone for the marginalization and systemic barriers faced during and after incarceration—social, psychological, and legal. Determined to succeed, I had to swallow my pride.

My first job was through a temp agency in the City of Riviera Beach's Public Works Department as a general laborer. Using my aquatic pesticide applicator license, I sprayed weeds in canals for $9.05 per hour. Despite the low pay, I was grateful after working for free in prison, knowing it was a start. Eventually, my pesticide licenses and CDL led to a full-time position as a spray technician with better pay and benefits. It wasn't easy; my background raised red flags in HR, and I was challenged for lacking one year of pesticide application experience.

After five months, the City hired me as the spray tech due to a shortage of licensed applicators. I seized every opportunity for certifications and professional development and, within 14 months, became interim manager for the Streets & Grounds Division. This promotion made me a target, with co-workers resenting me, especially since I'd been home for only 20 months. They didn't see the 10 years I spent preparing for opportunities. It bothered me at first, but my best friend's words resonated with me when he said, "Don't worry about them. Do what you have to do. Besides, they had a 25-year headstart on you, so f— them" (E. Adams, personal communication, 2018). Right then, I stopped apologizing for my success.

Breaking Chains, Building Futures

Malcolm, the operations manager, and Terrence, the interim director, played key roles in my career. Malcolm hired me full-time, and Terrence offered me an interim manager position on the condition that I pursue a degree. I accepted, knowing it was necessary for advancement. The City's tuition reimbursement program allowed me to earn my degree debt-free. Terrence still refers to me as part of his success story for recognizing my potential. I enrolled at Palm Beach Atlantic University, working by day and attending classes by night. Eventually I was reassigned back to my spray tech position, but I stayed determined. In December 2020, I graduated with honors in organizational leadership and, after interviewing in January, transferred to The Reentry Center in February to fulfill my purpose.

I transitioned into reentry work, a field I was passionate about. The director of The Reentry Center, Orie, had tried to recruit me for years, recognizing my unpaid community work. Although the position paid less, I chose purpose over money. This role has been fulfilling, allowing me to grow while making a meaningful impact. I'm blessed to now teach two classes at the same facility from which I was released in 2017. Two participants from my first Peer Mentoring class are now home and my co-workers. Talk about life coming full circle. I also credit my colleagues in the reentry community for helping me learn and grow as a professional. Even my pay has increased over time.

Continuing to grow professionally is a priority for me. While browsing LinkedIn, I discovered Prison to Professionals (P2P), which offers advanced training for system-impacted individuals. I joined cohort 28, and since then, P2P has helped me leverage my education, embrace my life story, and boost my confidence. The program inspired me to pursue a master's in criminal justice, but I encountered a roadblock with the application process. Instead, P2P guided me toward universities willing to work with system-impacted individuals. While I plan to pursue a master's later, my focus now is on creating intellectual properties, including books, professional development training, conflict resolution services, and organizational leadership coaching.

I'm grateful for opportunities to serve as president of the board of directors for the National Association of Reentry Professionals Inc. (NARP), as a member of the Palm Beach County Criminal Justice Commission, and as a voting member on the executive committee for the Palm Beach County Reentry Task Force.

Whenever possible, I conduct community mediations remotely for Just Mediation Pittsburgh, a nonprofit resolving housing disputes between landlords and tenants to prevent homelessness in Allegheny County, Pennsylvania.

Mentoring youth and young adults is one of the most fulfilling parts of my work. I'm developing a conflict resolution program to train them as certified mediators, empowering them to address bullying, harassment, and gang activity while promoting peaceful resolution and meaningful change.

I'm privileged to serve alongside organizations dedicated to the incarcerated and formerly incarcerated. Through P2P as a scholar and mentor, I empower system-impacted individuals via advocacy and policy initiatives. As an alumnus of JustLeadership USA's Leading with Conviction (LwC) Cohort 2024 and a member of the JustUS Coordinating Council (JCC) and the Florida Rights Restoration Coalition (FRRC), I strive to dismantle disenfranchisement, facilitate successful reentry, and curtail recidivism.

In 2024, a global faith-based organization excluded me from a peaceful communities panel due to my background. However, members of the United Nations created a separate panel on Criminal Justice & Inequalities in the Global Development Agenda, launching my global advocacy in New York. Through my organization,

Libra-Life International, I now lead criminal justice reform, forging strategic partnerships and influencing policy across North America, East Africa, and Western Europe.

Reflecting on my journey, I've learned that adversity can fuel growth and transformation. Early experiences with racial prejudice and educational injustice opened my eyes to systemic inequality, inspiring me to rise above and create change for others facing similar struggles. Education became my tool for empowerment, showing me that knowledge is not just power but a pathway to justice. Change requires both inner strength and external support, and through faith, education, and mentorship, I discovered my purpose. My healing journey is ongoing, but with each step, I grow stronger. To others facing hardships, remember: you are not defined by your circumstances. With courage and determination, you can overcome and inspire change. Choose purpose, and let your story light the way for others.

Oswald Newbold II

References

Farrington, D. P., & Welsh, B. C. (2007). *Saving children from a life of crime: Early risk factors and effective interventions*. Oxford University Press.

JNS. (2025, January 23). *Palm Beach County school district faces federal review of potential bias*. JNS. Retrieved February 12, 2025, from https://www.jns.org/palm-beach-county-school-district-faces-federal-review-of-potential-bias/.

McCray, C. L. (2022). *The Joseph anointing: From prison to prosperity*.

ProPublica. (n.d.). *Miseducation: How racial disparities affect student discipline in schools*. ProPublica. Retrieved February 12, 2025, from https://projects.propublica.org/miseducation/district/1201500.

Steinhardt, N. Y. U. (2016, August 29). *Equity audit: Palm Beach County School District final report*. Metro Center for Research on Equity and the Transformation of Schools. Retrieved February 12, 2025, from https://docs.steinhardt.nyu.edu/pdfs/metrocenter/atn293/reval/equity_audit_palm_beach_final_report_8_29_16.pdf.

United States Sentencing Commission (2017). *Demographic differences in sentencing: An update to the 2012 Booker report*. U.S. Sentencing Commission. https://www.ussc.gov/research/research-reports/demographic-differences-sentencing.

U.S. Const. amend. XIV, § 1 (1868).

Chapter 2

Light to Life: One Mission, One Voice—A Story of Resilience and Advocacy

By Tenaj Moody, MS, LBS

Introduction to Tenaj Moody's Chapter
By Stanley Andrisse

From the moment I first met Tenaj Moody, I was struck by her unyielding determination to transform her lived experiences into a catalyst for systemic change. Her journey from navigating the criminal legal system to founding Light to Life is a testament to her strength, vision, and unwavering commitment to empowering justice-impacted women and girls.

In Tenaj's words, her path was shaped by systemic barriers such as poverty and the criminalization of survival—a reality for many marginalized communities. But instead of succumbing to these challenges, she channeled her experiences into groundbreaking work, building culturally affirming, gender-responsive, and trauma-informed programs for survivors of gender-based violence (GBV). Through her leadership, Light to Life has become a beacon of hope, addressing the intersectionality of incarceration, trauma, and structural racism, and providing tools for self-awareness and empowerment to those most often overlooked.

(continued)

(continued)

Collaborating with Tenaj through Prison to Professionals (P2P) has been one of the most rewarding aspects of my work. Together, we've launched initiatives that have supported more than 500 justice-impacted women and girls nationwide. One of the most impactful projects we've undertaken was securing funding from Johns Hopkins University and Morgan CARES at Morgan State University to evaluate P2P's Womxn's Cohort, an initiative focused on gender-responsive, trauma-informed programming, mentoring, educational counseling, workforce development, and transitional housing. These efforts have demonstrated the transformative power of providing justice-impacted individuals with the resources and support to break cycles of violence and trauma.

Tenaj's story is not just about overcoming adversity; it's about rewriting the narrative. Her work challenges societal perceptions that often separate survivors from those entangled in the legal system, showcasing the necessity of addressing systemic injustices at their root. Through her advocacy, she has redefined what it means to be a leader in the fight for gender justice, and social justice, and her story is an inspiration to all who strive for equity and empowerment.

This chapter reflects Tenaj Moody's relentless dedication, resilience, and profound impact of her work—an enduring reminder that change is not just possible but inevitable when driven by purpose and passion.

Your story is what makes you unique. Your story is what makes you special; it's what makes you *you*. As the reader, you should know I didn't want to write a typical biography structuring my life from A to B. I share with you different moments and phases in my life that were pivotal in my growth as a person hoping that my lived experiences could resonate, change, or save someone's life.

I highly encourage you to share what you have learned with your friends and family and on social media to begin to shift the narrative on the different topics discussed and create an authentic community on the importance of storytelling and sharing your own story. Again, this is not your average biography, I'm not your average woman, and if you're reading, you're not average either—whether you have faced poverty, trauma, addiction, mental health challenges, racism, sexism, classism, or any other "isms," or you feel like you're missing something and searching for a place of understanding. Maybe you think this book isn't for you, but since you're a human being, I know you have struggled and faced adversity in your life. This is a friendly reminder that you're not alone. This is for anyone chasing a dream and trying to do what they can with what they have. This is for those everyday people who are just trying to do their best and be their best. For anyone who has ever doubted you and made you feel like you're not enough, I'm here to tell you, tell them to go screw themselves because you're more than enough. This is for anyone chasing a dream and trying to do what they can with what they have. This is for those *everyday people* who are just trying to do their best and be their best.

You don't need to go to an Ivy League college to be "intelligent" and be respected. You don't need to make six figures to be successful. Let's be clear: money or school is not an accurate metric for the totality of your human experiences and dopeness. This is for anyone who is resourceful and can make $20 stretch for an entire week. I'm writing this chapter to inspire, encourage, and uplift the often overshadowed and underestimated voices. This is about embracing who you are and who you're becoming, while carrying with you everything that has brought you here today. Embrace your past; do not be ashamed of it. I hope you find healing through my reflections as much as I have while writing this. I hope that you can learn and grow and not just "go through" shit in life but understand and appreciate your own lived experiences by practicing gratitude, knowing that no one can walk in your shoes, no one is like you, and you're doing a pretty good job at handling some heavy shit.

As you go on this journey with me, you will see that my thoughts are not one streamed line of consciousness but rather a road trip through moments in my life that brought me pain, joy, and lessons. I share these moments, hoping that it resonates with someone to let them know that I see you and that you should keep going. I also hope this book challenges you to think differently and makes you feel some discomfort, because that's a small indication that you may need to do some internal work to create meaningful change in your own life. Trust the process. Trust yourself. There are no ceilings; break that shit down. You can achieve anything you put your mind to with consistency, persistence, and commitment. Find power in your story.

The World Is Cruel to Women

> "Women have been mistreated for centuries; you don't need a history lesson to know that."
> — *Tenaj Moody*

From the beginning of time, Black women and women in general have not been protected, and instead, there has been this proclivity to characterize women as perpetrators of their own abuse. Why do we view a woman's victimization as a crime? Why are 79% of incarcerated women domestic violence victims and 60% are sexual abuse survivors? Why are 90% of women in prison today convicted of murder for defending themselves from a partner who has battered them?[1] These are the questions we should be asking. These statistics are more than just numbers; they're humans who are mothers, grandmothers, daughters, caregivers, and the rock to the family. We as a society, culture, and nation need to stop judging women when we are not even asking the right questions to understand their "why." We should be asking questions like: What led to your situation? What barriers have you faced that made it difficult to find support or resources? How have past experiences shaped the decisions you've made? Gender-responsive and trauma-informed questions like these allow us to see the person behind the statistics, giving them a voice and understanding their unique journey.

The 2024 Prison Policy[2] report on women's incarceration highlights that approximately 190,600 women are currently incarcerated in the United States. The report emphasizes that women, particularly Black and Hispanic women, are disproportionately affected by incarceration, with 17% of incarcerated women being Black and 19% Hispanic. Many women are held in local jails, often unconvicted, leading to dire consequences for their health and family dynamics. Additionally, a significant portion of incarcerated women face issues like homelessness, mental health problems, and a lack of access to adequate healthcare.

It's far too common how these kinds of experiences are exploited in the media and how these women and young women are criminalized for their victimization. There is an intersectionality between gender, race, incarceration, and domestic violence. We see it throughout history and events today. The history of violence against and brutality of women is often overlooked and misunderstood. Black women in the early 1660s were raped, and the men (specifically white men) were not held accountable; in fact, it wasn't even considered rape by law. A quick history lesson: part of the Virginia Slave Laws incentivized the forced sexual acts against Black women, intending to have their offspring serve as slaves (Gross, p. 3). In other words, this is historical evidence to prove women were being forced to have sex and men were being incentivized for it during the 1600s, which is modern-day sex trafficking.

These data points are only to share with you to understand the intersectionality of gender, race, domestic violence, and incarceration. These statistics do not provide you with a complete picture of the unique impact of mass incarceration on women and why women are the fastest growing population in jails and prisons. Celia was an enslaved Black woman who in 1855 defended herself from a sexual assault by her enslaver and was hung in Missouri. Inez Garcia was a Latina women who defended herself from a rape in 1974 and spent two years in Soledad State Penitentiary. CeCe McDonald is a transgender Black woman who in 2011 fought for her life against a racist and transphobic attack and was forced to serve 19 months in a male prison. Marissa Alexander, a Black woman, was prosecuted in 2012 and served three years behind bars and two years in house detention while being forced to wear and pay for a surveillance ankle monitor for defending herself against her abusive husband.

What do all of these women have in common? These women were courageous enough to fight for their own dignity knowing they could be punished or murdered for simply being a victim. These women serve as inspiration for many young women and girls like me to fight for justice and be victors, not simply victims.

My intention is to raise awareness on this issue and speak about the inequalities women face in our world to ensure all women of all races and especially women of color are not left out of the conversation. We need to continue fighting for women; we need to have real policy reform and end mass incarceration and begin rehabilitation upon entry and reentry.

Women in prison are usually an afterthought when in conversations about men and incarceration, but it shouldn't be that way. Now don't get me wrong men, specifically Black men, are disproportionately affected by the carceral system. However, we cannot ignore that women are the fastest-growing correctional population in the United States. Women have faced societal and historical disadvantages. This is part of the reason that I have made it my life's work to be an advocate and an activist for women, survivors, and women who have been criminalized due to their victimization. There is no justice in our system when we do not seek to find the truth, hold people accountable, provide fair sentences or appropriate programming/treatment. When it comes down to it, this is not just a women's issue. This is everybody's issue. We're all part of the problem if we choose to ignore it. This is a gender, race-based, and socioeconomic problem that our society and politics have decided to ignore and instead use punishment as a form of rehabilitation.

At the age of 14, my mom ran away because of the abuse and mistreatment in her home. She became a victim of human trafficking, which led to her incarceration. Despite the odds against her and the collateral effects of incarceration, she fought and prevailed. In a similar vein, at 16, I believed I found the love of my life. Looking back, I realize that while it felt like true love, it was also a moment of youthful naivety, shaped by the complexities of my past and childhood. I was arrested for defending myself, put on probation, and needed to pay fines. Unfortunately, I was not viewed as a victim by our legal system, and I had no evidence of the abuse that happened to me for three years. I, too, was criminalized for my victimization. I knew from that point moving forward, I would never let anyone gain power and control over my life the way my abuser did.

I know I'm not the only one in life who has felt misunderstood, weak, vulnerable, powerless, and voiceless. My mission in life is to ensure we dismantle the myths around women's incarceration and the stereotypes that people are quick to place on others when they haven't walked in their shoes. My mother is the most intelligent person I have ever met. She knows how to survive whatever life throws at her. I don't see my mom as another statistic; she is my mother, a strong, beautiful, outspoken person with a big heart full of love. I genuinely believe it is an honor for me to witness the true meaning of what it means to be "resilient" through her lived testimony. She is one of the reasons why I'm a victor and not a victim.

I'm fortunate enough to have lived to tell my story and decide how I want to rewrite my story. I took my power back. In 2011, I found a place of healing and understood that I was not the only one who had experienced an abusive relationship at such a young age. I felt motivated to create a community where other young people who may have had similar experiences could have a place to break their silence and become empowered through education. This is when I decided to create Light to Life as the first funded domestic violence prevention program on Wesley College's campus. Light to Life's mission is to educate, empower, and engage communities to prevent gender-based violence. Light to Life fulfills this mission by providing gender-responsive, culturally-affirming, trauma-informed programming, technical assistance, and consulting tailored to survivors of gender-based violence (GBV), women, girls, gender nonconforming (GNC) people, and justice-involved women and girls.

I believe what sets us apart is our ability to create safe spaces. We're able to cultivate a supportive community in-person or virtually that teaches, guides, and equips survivors, justice-involved women, girls, and gender-expansive youth through a journey of self-awareness. Light to Life provides international gender-responsive support and trauma-informed programming through digital resources, leadership opportunities, and educational workshops. By speaking my truth and breaking the silence, I found my "light to life." Light to Life became my therapy; everyone's healing journey is different. For me, I healed by sharing my story and helping others. Since 2011, I have been able to use my story as a catalyst to drive my passion for educating, empowering, and engaging communities in a movement to prevent domestic violence. Through the power of sharing my story, I have been able to impact more than 1,700 college students and 500+ system-impacted women and girls across different states. Now, I'm 32 years old; the founder and program director of Light to Life, a three-time award-winning social enterprise dedicated to preventing gender-based violence; an internationally renowned educator; a keynote speaker on domestic violence, sexual violence, the criminal legal system, and mental health; a two-time best-selling author; and a licensed behavior specialist with a master's degree in criminal justice. My lived experiences have been a catalyst that drive my dedicated career to human services, the criminal legal system, and victim advocacy. I'm not saying this to brag; I am providing you with proof that anything is possible when you believe in yourself, have a passion, have mentors and support, and keep moving forward.

Society and our legal system does not look at all survivors the same. As you read everyone's stories, I want you to challenge the idea that "survivors" and "people who have committed crimes" are two diametrically opposed groups. I want you to reflect and think, how do we view a woman's victimization? As a crime? Is it their fault?

There is no justice in our system or in our world when we do not seek to find the truth. This is not just a women's issue, a minority issue, or a poor people's problem; the current state of our nation is everyone's problem, and if we choose to ignore it, the future of American families will be the ones to suffer. Justice for women and girls is about building safe, inclusive spaces where women can heal, have a connection to community through sisterhood, learn and grow, and return to their families with the tools and knowledge to feel empowered in their everyday lives.

Justice for women and girls like Marissa Alexander, Inez Garcia, Celia, CeCe Mcdonald, and my mom should be celebrated for their strength and recognized for their resilience and the audacity to fight back even when the odds are stacked against them. Justice is about centering the voices of justice-impacted women and girls to improve reentry programming, transform policies, and provide resources.

I hope by sharing this with you, it can begin to challenge your perspective on how we view and treat women in our world. If you have never been a victim, been a survivor, witnessed violence in your home, been incarcerated, had a parent or family member who was incarcerated, or felt like you have a scarlet letter embroidered in your identity, please sit down, be quiet, listen without judging, and educate yourself on these topics and issues.

If someone doesn't believe you, speak your truth anyway. Do not be silent; instead, shout. If someone does not see your honest character, blind them with your light. Never give up on yourself, and understand your story is not something to be ashamed of. Your story is what makes you a resilient, strong, compassionate, empathetic, and intelligent woman. Your story of strength is what motivates, inspires, encourages, and influences real change in this world. Your voice is what drives the mission to continuously fight for women who are unable to fight for themselves. Please know that you're not alone in your journey. We're here, I am here, and I do not plan on leaving this fight until we have won. I live to see the day when women's voices are amplified, when women's testimonies are no longer an afterthought, when women's voices are centered in conversations that involve them instead of just men. Please stay strong, put your head up, and keep moving forward! Do not look back because you're not going there anymore.

I encourage you all to be part of this mission by sharing these stories and information in your communities to uplift women and girls who are impacted by the legal system and are also victors.

Informational Resources

I know my survivor story is much bigger than me, and I understand domestic violence is a silent epidemic. I know preparing to leave an abusive situation takes quiet strength and courage and can cause many heartaches, especially if you did love your partner at one point, but this is about you and your safety; remember that. When preparing to leave, keep in mind some of these tips/tools.

Creating a safety plan is one of the most important tools to know about because it is important for anyone experiencing domestic violence or preparing to leave. A safety plan is personalized based on your physical and emotional needs.

How to Prepare a Safety Plan

1. Document all evidence of the abuse, record dates, take pictures, and record any threats made to you; write this in a journal or keep it in a small safety lockbox somewhere where only you can find it.
2. Establish a plan where you can run for safety if you need to and only let someone you trust know where that place is.
3. Try to set money aside or save a little bit of money and ask a trusted friend or family to hold on to the money for when you need it.
4. Create a safety word that only you and a trusted friend or family know about; for example, "eagles" could be a signal that you're in danger and can be texted immediately to someone to know you need help.

Once you find the courage and strength to leave, there are a few things to make sure you don't forget to bring with you.

Light to Life: One Mission, One Voice

Check off the items on this list to make sure you have all these important documents to turn over a new leaf:

Identification

- Driver's license or state ID card
- Birth certificate and children's birth certificates
- Social security cards
- Financial information
- Money and/or credit cards (in your name)
- Checking and savings account books

Legal Paperwork

- A protective order, if applicable (make multiple copies if possible)
- Copies of any lease or rental agreements or the deed to your home
- Car registration and insurance papers
- Health and life insurance papers
- Medical records for you and your children
- School records
- Work permits/green cards/visas
- Passport
- Any legal documents, including divorce and custody paper

Emergency Numbers

- Your attorney
- Your local domestic violence program or shelter

- Trusted friends and family members
- Your local doctor's office and hospital
- Criminal legal resources
- Hotline number

Other Important Stuff

- Medications and refills (if possible)
- Emergency items like food, bottles of water, and a first aid kit
- Multiple changes of clothes
- Emergency money
- Address book
- Extra sets of house and car keys
- Pictures and sentimental items
- Valuable items, such as jewelry

Creating a safety plan takes time, and there is support to help you or a friend safely make these plans. There are plenty of advocates and hotline numbers you can create a plan with if this is something you believe will be helpful for you. Please note, this safety plan may not be applicable to every person as each has different circumstances, such as being married or having kids/pets. Regardless of the circumstances, it is important to be aware of what a safety plan is.

If this was not helpful for you, check out these other great programs that support survivors of domestic violence. Of course, you always have my program Light to Life as a resource too.

Domestic Violence Resources

- www.Lighttolife.org, onemissiononevoice@gmail.com
- www.Loveisrespect.org, text: LOVEIS to 1.866.331.9474, call 1.866.331.9474
- www.thehotline.org, call 1.800.799.SAFE (7233)
- www.onelovefoundation.org

How to Help a Friend

Suppose you have a friend or family member experiencing domestic violence and they're just not ready to leave or maybe have left and returned to their partner multiple times. Let's first start with the following to help your friend:

1. Educate yourself to know the warning signs and the relationship spectrum.
2. Express your concern by letting them know you care about them and reassuring them they're not alone.
3. Let your friend know they can count on you when they need to; stay patient and supportive. This is important because sometimes it can take a person seven to eight times until your friend is ready to leave. Let's face it; some things are just easier said than done.
4. Being patient and supportive can go a long way; trust me, even if your friend may not thank you for it right away, your support will not go unnoticed, and you can potentially save their life.
5. Share educational resources with them when they're ready to dive into it; this is just another gesture to simply express to your friend your concern and support for them.

6. Take care of yourself while helping your friend or family. There is such a thing called *vicarious trauma* and *compassion fatigue*. To put it simply, vicarious trauma is when you're witness to hearing or seeing something traumatic. Compassion fatigue happens when a person begins to take on another person's problems as your own. This can cause a significant burden, stress, and even depression if you do not practice self-care.

This is why it's essential to prioritize yourself and practice self-care. It can look different for many people; the one thing that is the same for everyone in whatever activity you decide to engage in for your self-care should relieve stress and enhance your physical and emotional well-being. It's important to note your stressors/triggers to practice self-care effectively to be preventive rather than reactive in those situations. Make sure to identify your stressors first and then apply what coping strategies you will practice to overcome those triggers.

If you know someone who has been a victim of domestic violence or human trafficking, please share these national resources:

Other Resources

National Domestic Violence Hotline:

Call 1-800-799-7233 or 1-800-787-3224 for TTY, or if you're unable to speak safely, you can log onto thehotline.org or text LOVEIS to 22522.

National Human Trafficking Hotline: 1 (888) 373-7888 or (Text "HELP" or "INFO").

Tenaj Moody at a book signing for one of her previous books, *Carry It with You*, c. 2021

Chapter 3

Lessons Beyond the Classroom: An Educator's Journey of Resilience, Redemption, and Purpose

By Dr. Brian Metcalf

Introduction to Dr. Brian Metcalf's Chapter

By Dr. Stanley Andrisse

I remember the first time I met Dr. Brian Metcalf. It was at an event at Rush University, one of those moments where the air is thick with potential—where the weight of stories, untold and unfolding, fills the room. He was standing near the back, listening, absorbing. When we finally spoke, I could see it in his eyes—that mix of brilliance and burden, the way the system had touched him but hadn't taken him.

"I don't even know where to begin," he said.

I knew that feeling. That fog. The way the world stops seeing you for your mind and starts seeing you for your past—or worse, a version of you they've constructed in their own minds. The degrees don't matter. The work you've done and the hours you've poured into becoming something greater don't matter. The system sees only what it wants to see.

But I also knew something else—how to move through that, how to reclaim the narrative.

(continued)

(continued)

"Begin where it started," I told him. "Begin where you knew you were more than the system wanted you to believe."

Brian had become an impactful leader in Chicago before the legal system ever laid its hands on him. He wasn't supposed to be here, standing in the spaces reserved for the forgotten. And yet, there he was. An educator. A thinker. A man who had spent years sharpening his mind and others, only to be told that the world would now define him by his lowest moment.

But the thing about Brian—the thing about all of us who have faced that reckoning—is that we are more than our moments. More than the worst thing we've done, more than the labels they try to affix to us. That's what Prison to Professionals (P2P) was built for—to remind us that we are not statistics, not broken, not irredeemable.

When Brian connected with P2P, I saw the shift happen in real time. It wasn't about me. It wasn't even about P2P, really. It was about recognition—seeing yourself reflected in someone who had made it through.

"It's different when you see it in real life," he told me later. "When you see someone who actually walked through it and came out on the other side."

I nodded. Because I knew.

What follows is Brian's story—one of perseverance, of reclaiming his future, of refusing to let the world dictate who he could be. This is not just his story; this is the story of so many of us. And if you listen closely, you might just hear your own voice in it too.

Background and Early Life

I was born into a world already weighted with secrets. My mother—a woman of deep contradictions, of warmth and silence, of sacrifice and struggle—raised five children on her own. She had some college education but not enough to keep poverty from curling around us like an unshakable shadow. And then there was me—the odd one out, the child with a different father, a different story etched into my existence before I was even old enough to understand it. All of our fathers were married to other women, leaving my mother with nothing but the fractured pieces of their choices and the burden of five children to raise in a house that never had enough.

But my mother was not alone. My aunt, a quiet force of stability, lived with us, a second maternal figure trying to make up for what life had denied us. Yet, despite her presence, the absence of certainty, of security, pressed down on us every day. And my mother—God bless her—was battling demons none of us could name at the time. Anxiety. Depression. Bipolar disorder. Some days, she was all light and laughter, wrapping us in the warmth of her love. Other days, she withdrew into herself, a ghost in our home, leaving us desperate to pull her back into our world.

We learned early that attention from her was a rare commodity, and each of us found different ways to grasp at it. For me, it was school. If I did well, if I brought home the right grades, if I played the part of the perfect child, then I could hold her gaze a little longer, hear her voice filled with pride rather than exhaustion.

"That's my doctor," she would say, smiling. "That's my Brian."

She would look at my siblings, eyes filled with expectation, and say, "Why can't you be like him?"

And just like that, my success became the wedge that separated me from them. I was the golden child, the one who did everything "right," but even I knew it wasn't true. I was simply the one who learned how to perform for love.

But it was my brother who taught me about the failings of the world. He was brilliant—a natural when it came to math and science—but he wasn't built for sitting still, for folding his hands on a desk and following rules that suffocated him. He needed movement, space, freedom. And when the system couldn't give him that, when it tried to force him into a box too small for his spirit, I watched the light in his eyes flicker and fade.

By the time I was preparing for college, he was heading to prison. Armed robbery. A boy with an uncontainable energy that no one knew how to nurture. The world saw him as a problem to be disciplined, not a mind to be understood. And I knew, deep in my soul, that it wasn't just his choices that led him there—it was the system's failure to see him for who he was.

That was when I knew.

I didn't want another Black boy to sit in a classroom where he was misunderstood. I didn't want another child to be punished for learning differently. I didn't want the streets or the prison system to be the only paths available to those who weren't given the space to thrive. I would become an educator, not just to teach but to fight—to create spaces where kids like my brother could be seen, valued, and set free from the limitations the world tried to place on them.

I threw myself into teaching with a passion that left little room for anything else. I swore I would retire from it, convinced that the classroom was where I could do the best. And for a while, that was true.

Chicago. A summer school classroom. A 100-degree day with no air conditioning, the kind of heat that wraps itself around your bones and dares you to focus on anything but survival. But there they were—my students. Black kids from the projects, the ones the world had already decided were lost causes, sitting in my classroom every single day, never missing a session.

It wasn't discipline that kept them coming back. It wasn't fear. It was engagement. It was respect. It was the way I made the lessons feel like they belonged to them. Spanish wasn't just a subject—it was a tool, a connection to the world they wanted to be part of. They learned how to order food, how to introduce themselves, how to ask someone on a date in Spanish. "Can you teach me how to ask out a Mexican girl?" one of my boys asked, and we did just that. Learning became real, alive, necessary.

The district took notice. A woman named Carol Briggs came to my class, suspicious of the 100% attendance rate. She left astonished. "You need to be a school administrator," she told me. "These kids need you on a larger scale."

I resisted at first. The classroom was where I had the most direct impact. It was where I could shield my students from policies that didn't serve them. But she was right. I could fight harder, change more, reach further if I stepped into leadership. And so I did.

I took schools that were failing and turned them into places where Black and brown kids excelled. Literacy, math, and science scores soared in neighborhoods where they said it wasn't possible. We proved them wrong. And with those rising scores came resources, funding, recognition—things that should have been given freely but had to be earned through relentless proof of our worth.

Before my legal challenges, that was my biggest impact—creating schools where our children weren't just surviving but thriving. And yet, even with all I had built, all the barriers I had broken, the past had a way of circling back, of demanding payment for sins I thought I had outrun.

But transformation doesn't come from an unbroken path. It comes from fire, from loss, from the moments that strip us bare and force us to rebuild. My story—like so many of ours—isn't just one of success. It is one of redemption, of resilience, of proving, again and again, that we are more than the circumstances that seek to define us.

And I am still here. Still fighting. Still proving that our stories don't end in the places where the world expects them to.

Educational Journey

I was born into a world that didn't expect much of me. Not because I wasn't brilliant, not because I didn't have the potential to change the very foundation of the spaces I entered—but because I was Black, because I was gay, because I was meant to fit into the narrow mold society had carved out for me. And yet, against the weight of those expectations, I carved out a different path. One that would take me from student to educator, from observer to leader, from a dream deferred to a reality redefined.

When I first started teaching in 1997, I knew I wanted to do more. Teaching was noble, necessary, but I wanted to be in a position to shift systems, to disrupt cycles of failure that had been set in motion long before my students ever walked through those doors. By 2003, I had started researching what it took to become an administrator. That's when I learned about the Type 75, the administrator's license issued by the Illinois State Board of Education. The pathway was clear: I needed a master's in educational leadership to get there.

So I enrolled at Governors State University, making the drive four days a week, sacrificing time, rest, and whatever was left of my social life. It should have taken two years, but life has a way of stretching out timelines. By 2006, I had my Type 75, and doors that had once been padlocked started to open.

My first role as a district-level administrator was in the Office of Specialized Services, a department responsible for students with disabilities. My job was to be a liaison between schools and families, a bridge where there had once been a chasm. Too often, these families—predominantly Black, marginalized, unheard—were met with bureaucratic indifference when they sought the services their children were legally entitled to. I became their advocate, their translator in a language of power they had never been taught to speak.

But even as I fought for these families, I knew my work was far from done. In 2009, I became an assistant principal at the largest elementary school in Chicago, a behemoth of a building with 1,500 students and 210 staff members. The school was failing, and not in the way they mark numbers on a sheet. It was failing its students, its families, its community. I was sent there because they needed someone who understood instruction, someone who could translate data into real change.

The first year, we improved science scores by 14%, reading by 12%, and math by 13%. In a school where failure had once been expected, we redefined success. But change is never comfortable, and just as I had settled into my role, the district had other plans.

On April 4—Report Card Pickup Day—I was called into the office. "Tomorrow, you'll be the principal of another school," they told me. No warning, no transition, just an expectation that I would walk into another struggling school and do what I did best: fix it.

For four years, I led that school, and for four years, we transformed it. The teachers, the students, the community—together, we made it work. I had finally found my rhythm, my home. And then the district came calling again.

This time, they wanted me to take over one of the most dangerous high schools in the city. I resisted. I had earned my comfort, I had built something sustainable, and I was tired. But when the mayor's office got involved, when they told me this was bigger than one school, that this was about proving what was possible—how could I say no?

So I stepped into a school with 110 students in a building meant for 2,000. A school surrounded by seven elementary schools, none of which fed into it because parents would rather send their children across the city than risk their safety there. It wasn't just a school—it was a symbol of failure, of fear, of everything wrong with a system that had long since stopped serving the people who needed it most.

The first thing I did was remove the police officers from the hallways, tucking them into a back room where they couldn't loom over students like shadows of oppression. I took down the metal detectors, stripped away the institutionalized hostility that greeted students at the door. People called me crazy, but I knew what I was doing. These kids weren't criminals. They were firecrackers—full of energy, full of potential, just waiting for someone to believe in them.

We introduced restorative practices—peace circles, conflict resolution, full-time counselors dedicated to breaking generational trauma instead of perpetuating it. Within a year, discipline infractions plummeted. The fights that once defined the school became the exception, not the rule. The students started to believe in the school, in themselves. And that, more than any test score, was the victory I had been fighting for.

Education was never just about books and grades. It was about survival, about resilience, about the power of transformation. It was about proving that no matter where you start, no matter what barriers are placed in your way, you can still rise. I had spent my entire career fighting to make that truth a reality—not just for myself but for every student who had ever been told they weren't enough.

And in doing so, I found my own transformation. I was no longer just an educator, no longer just an administrator. I was a witness to change, a catalyst for redemption, and proof that impact is measured not in accolades, but in lives changed.

I had seen the way the world moved, and I knew that no man rises without the weight of his own determination pressing against him. In 2016, when I was named chief of schools, I stood at the edge of something vast, something trembling with possibility. I did not need a doctorate to hold that title, but need and desire are different beasts. I had my eyes on something greater—a superintendency, a place at the table where decisions shaped the futures of children who looked like me, who walked the same streets I once did. And so I studied the landscape and saw how the power was arranged, how credentials were the currency of entry. I knew I could stand on my experience, on my numbers, but so could they. And so I would take no chances; I would match them step for step. In 2017, I walked through the doors of National Louis University, knowing that the journey ahead was not about the degree itself, but about what it would allow me to do. By June 2019, I had the paper, Ed.D in educational leadership, but more than that, I had the weight of my own will behind me, ready to carve a way forward. Armed with my new credentials and a sense of purpose, I was about to face a new set of hurdles—ones that were deeply embedded in the complexities of our legal system, which would require a different kind of resolve.

Legal System Involvement

I never saw it coming. I never thought my desire to help would lead me into the tangled web of the legal system. I was always the one to say yes, to be there when someone needed me, to make sure the people in my life never felt abandoned the way I had. That was my weakness, my fatal flaw. And when my friend—let's call her Angela—came to me, desperate, drowning in financial turmoil, I did what I always did. I helped.

At first, it seemed harmless. She needed work. I had the means to help her, or so I thought. "I can file paperwork for you," she had said. And it wasn't unusual; people do odd jobs all the time. It felt like a favor, one friend helping another, but then she stopped showing up. The work wasn't getting done, but the money was still flowing, her excuses as plentiful as the invoices I kept approving. I told myself I was just being understanding, just being kind. But kindness turned into complicity, and complicity turned into crime.

When the money became too much, when the cycle kept repeating, I knew I had to stop. But stopping isn't always as easy as it seems. Angela pleaded, insisted. She had children, dreams, a future she was trying to build. And I was trapped between my conscience and my need to be the person who didn't let people down. Then came Eric—her boyfriend or fiancé or husband-to-be—another name on another invoice, another excuse to keep the whole thing rolling forward. And still, I told myself it wasn't that bad. Until the day their accountant came knocking.

I didn't know him well, not personally. But he knew enough. He had seen the numbers, traced the money, put the puzzle together. And he wanted in. The moment he made his demand, I knew—I was caught. I could feel the walls closing in, the inevitability of it all washing over me. But the damage had already been done. The investigation began, and I had no choice but to face what was coming.

The day I realized I was under federal investigation was the day my life as I knew it ended. Everything I had built, everything I had worked for, was now tainted by a mistake I couldn't take back. For the first time in my life, I questioned my purpose, my place in the world. I had always believed I was meant to serve, to uplift, to fight for the marginalized. That belief had carried me through years of struggle and had defined who I was as an educator, as a mentor. But now? Now I was the one who needed saving.

I thought the future had already been decided for me. A job at a fast-food restaurant. A long-haul truck driver's license. A life spent on the fringes, where society puts people like me—people with a record, with a past. It wasn't just about punishment; it was about erasure. The world had already decided I was done. But I wasn't ready to accept that. Not yet.

It was during those long nights of uncertainty, when I was staring into the abyss of what my life had become, that I found P2P. A Google search, a desperate attempt to find someone—anyone—who had been through what I was going through. And there it was: a community, a lifeline, proof that my story wasn't over. I joined Cohort 28, and for the first time since my indictment, I saw something I hadn't allowed myself to believe in: possibility.

P2P wasn't just a program. It was a revelation. Here were people like me—brilliant, ambitious, once written off by the system, now rebuilding their lives. And not just rebuilding but thriving. Doctors, scholars, leaders. Men and women who had walked through the fire and come out stronger on the other side. And in them, I saw myself.

It was through P2P that I met Dr. Andrisse, who invited me into spaces I never thought I'd be welcomed in again. I remember stepping into Rush Hospital, seeing a room full of aspiring Black doctors, young men and women who looked like me, who shared my story. In that moment, I knew. This was it. This was my second chance.

But second chances don't come easy. The world still sees the record before it sees the man. I knew I needed a plan, a new path that allowed me to fulfill my purpose without the barriers that kept people like me out. Medicine called to me—not just as a profession, but as a responsibility. My mother had battled breast cancer, my sister colon cancer. I had seen firsthand how Black and brown people were treated in the healthcare system, how their pain was ignored, their concerns dismissed. I couldn't stand by and watch it happen again.

At first, I thought I'd become a physician assistant. But every program required that students refrain from working—a luxury I couldn't afford. So I adjusted, adapted. A nurse practitioner, a DNP—that was my new goal. It would allow me to diagnose, to prescribe, to heal. To fight the same fight I had always fought, but now with more purpose than ever before.

The legal system tried to define me. Tried to strip me of my future, my dreams. But I refused to let it. I wasn't just my worst mistake. I was a man with a purpose, with a calling. And with the support of P2P, I was ready to answer that call.

The road ahead wasn't easy. It still isn't. But I walk it with my head high, knowing that my story isn't one of defeat, but of redemption. Of transformation. Of impact. And I know that I am not alone.

My journey through the legal system changed me, but it did not break me. Instead, it strengthened my resolve to serve, to uplift, to be the person I was always meant to be. I am Dr. Brian Metcalf, and my story is far from over.

Personal Growth and Redemption

There was a time when I thought redemption was for other people. The ones who made the right mistakes, the ones whose sins were soft enough to be washed away with a few apologies and a fresh start. I didn't think I had that kind of luck. When you've been through the system—truly through it, your name inked into case files, your future a thing debated in courtrooms—you learn that some stains don't wash out easy. The world will remind you, over and over, that you are not to be trusted. That you are to be watched. That your past is the only truth they'll ever believe about you.

But I also learned that redemption is not given. It is taken. It is built with hands that shake but do not break.

P2P was a lifeline, yes. An organization, but more than that—a family, a whispered reminder that I was not alone. There were days when the weight of it all—judgments from strangers, doubts from within—threatened to pull me under. On those days, I picked up the phone. Basha, the director of equity at P2P, would answer, steady as ever, and remind me: I've been there too. And here's what you need to do next. It wasn't just the knowledge that mattered, though that was invaluable. It was the knowing. Knowing that someone else had survived this, that someone else had walked this same road and still found light at the end.

But even with support, there was the matter of myself. The quiet work of forgiving the man in the mirror. My therapist helped with that. She knew my story—the whole of it, the pieces I wished I could rewrite. She helped me untangle the guilt, helped me see that moving forward did not mean erasing the past, but carrying it differently. Lighter, with purpose instead of shame.

And then came the challenge of rebuilding. People love a redemption story until it shows up at their doorstep asking for a job, for a second chance, for something beyond pity. I knew what was waiting for me out there: the closed doors, the polite rejections, the silent judgments. I was lucky—my boss understood. He knew what it was to be justice-impacted. But I knew, too, that my story was not the norm. For so many of us, the barriers are built high and thick, and no amount of good intentions will tear them down. That's where purpose came in.

Purpose was not a thing I found all at once. It was something that revealed itself in small moments—the way I felt standing at Rush University, listening to Dr. Andrisse speak, realizing that maybe I, too, had something to give. It was in the conversations I had with other P2P scholars, in the times I felt myself slipping and someone else pulled me back. It was in the simple truth that staying connected, staying engaged, kept me believing in the possibility of more.

Some days, I still fight the doubt. But I also know this: I am not the man they wrote about in those court documents. I am more. And every day, I am writing a new story.

Transformation and Legacy

I was always reaching, stretching myself thin across an endless horizon, always thinking five, 10 years out, convinced that success was a finish line somewhere in the distance. I measured my worth in milestones—degrees, titles, the number of students I helped shape into something greater than themselves. But then the system marked me, and suddenly, the horizon shrank to a pinprick of light at the end of a long, dark corridor. I had to learn a new way to move, to measure success not in leaps, but in steady, deliberate steps.

For so long, I thought I had to prove something to the world, to carve out space where I could stand tall, unchallenged. But what I wish I had known then, what I would whisper to my younger self if given the chance, is that I was enough. Just as I was. I didn't owe the world an explanation, an apology, or an appeasement. I didn't need to bend myself into shapes that fit others' expectations. That lesson would have saved me years of anguish, of chasing validation that was never mine to hold.

The world will try to convince you that one mistake defines you. That one moment of weakness, one lapse in judgment, one regrettable decision is all you'll ever be. But that's a lie. The truth is, transformation is a choice. It's a daily practice. You don't have to surrender your dreams because the world says you're unworthy. You just have to surround yourself with people who remind you that you still belong to something greater. That's what justice-impacted folks need to hear—redemption isn't granted, it's reclaimed.

And to the educators who meet people like me on the other side, I say this: remember that we are human. Before that mistake, before that record, before that sentence, we were members of your classrooms, your communities. We were you. And we are still you. The measure of your impact is not in how you judge us, but in how you welcome us back. One conversation, one decision, one moment of grace can be the difference between someone believing in their own future or surrendering to despair. Be the difference.

I want more than words. I want policy and legislation that clears the path for professionals like me to step back into purpose without having to crawl over endless obstacles. The X's marked against us don't fade just because we've done the work. The barriers to employment, to education, to simply living with dignity—they remain. And that must change. Opportunity shouldn't be the exception; it should be the standard.

Programs like P2P save lives, not just by offering second chances but by walking beside us as we step into them. Because the truth is, when you re-enter, you are reborn into an unfamiliar world. Old ties unravel. The life you built before—friends, career, identity—is gone. And you must build again. That's what P2P gave me: a blueprint for a future I thought was lost. I remember standing at that conference at Rush, unsure of what came next. Drive a truck, maybe? But then I looked around, saw the people who had walked this road before me, and I knew—this is it. This is where I start again.

Success isn't about what's waiting at the end. It's about the step you take right now, in this moment. And right now, I am here. I am moving. I am building anew.

Chapter 4

Reentry Is Reinvention

By Judith Negron

Introduction to Judith Negron's Chapter
By Dr. Stanley Andrisse

Judith Negron's story is a powerful testament to resilience, transformation, and the drive to uplift others through shared experiences. When I first connected with Judith, her passion for creating meaningful change in the lives of justice-impacted individuals was immediately apparent. Her journey, marked by perseverance in the face of systemic barriers, highlights the need for comprehensive solutions to address the root causes of incarceration.

Judith's chapter explores critical themes such as mental health and substance abuse, education inequity, and the lack of rehabilitation programs—all key drivers that contribute to the cycle of incarceration. Her personal experience with these issues, combined with her dedication to helping others succeed in their reentry journey, makes her story deeply impactful.

Through Prison to Professionals (P2P), Judith has utilized the resources, support, and opportunities provided to her not only to

(continued)

> *(continued)*
>
> advance her own goals but to inspire and empower others. Her accomplishments, particularly her commitment to guiding others on their reentry path, embody the mission of P2P and demonstrate the transformative power of community and opportunity.
>
> Judith's chapter is a beacon of hope and a call to action, shedding light on the systemic challenges faced by many and the profound potential for redemption and reinvention.

Walking out of prison was surreal. My heart was a storm of emotions—discharge papers in hand, unspeakable gratitude for a surprise clemency, anticipation and eagerness for freedom and immense confidence in my readiness to begin again. I believed the road to reentry would be straightforward. After all, I had spent my life building skills, earning degrees, and becoming a professional. I had faith in the support of my family and friends, who stood unwaveringly by me through my incarceration. Having all the tools of education, decades of professional experience, and a steadfast support system; what could go wrong?

As it turns out, almost everything. I wasn't just reentering society; I was learning to navigate a world that had fundamentally changed in my absence. This is the reality many justice-impacted individuals face—a reality shaped by systemic barriers, societal judgment, and the lingering stigma of incarceration.

Reentry is not a return to normalcy. It is not a reset to the life you once had. Instead, it is a reckoning with an unrelenting system, one that reduces you to your criminal record, erasing your humanity, accomplishments, and potential. Reentry forces you to reinvent yourself—not because you want to but because you have no other choice.

This chapter is not just about my story. It is about what reentry has taught me about resilience, advocacy, and the transformative power of reinvention.

Breaking the Stereotype: My Journey to Incarceration

Mine is not your typical story, one that is marked by a traumatic childhood experience, exposed to drugs, poverty, abuse, neglect, lack of resources, or other commonly attributing factors or adverse childhood experiences (ACEs), leading to incarceration. I didn't grow up in poverty or experience the trauma that often creates a pipeline to the criminal justice system. No, this is not that story. This story is that of a first-generation immigrant family who worked tirelessly to give me a life filled with opportunity. I embraced those opportunities, earning a master's degree, building a thriving career as a licensed mental health professional, and attaining a comfortable middle-class life. I was the embodiment of the American dream—or so I thought. Even my education, spotless career, strong ethics, and stable life could not shield me from the complexities of a legal system that often views people through a binary lens. Thus, I found myself inside a prison cell!

My name is Judith Negron, and I am a mother, a wife, a daughter, and a sister. I am also one of the many formerly incarcerated Hispanics in this country. I was charged with a first-time nonviolent, white-collar offense and received a draconian sentence of 35 years plus three years of probation. This sentence was as arbitrary as it was draconian, a reflection of systemic disparities in sentencing laws rather than the severity of my own actions. This shocking turn of events forced me to confront the vulnerabilities within the justice system and within myself.

Finally, the injustices of my case were acknowledged when I received presidential clemency in 2020. This unbelievable gift gave me a second chance at life, and because of this, I strive every day to make the most of this once-in-a-lifetime opportunity.

However, receiving clemency after 10 years from my arrest was both a blessing and a curse: a blessing for the second chance it afforded me and a curse for the weight of proving I was worthy of it.

The abruptness of my fall from grace left me grappling with questions of identity. Who was I, if not the accomplished professional I had once been? How would I navigate a society that saw only my criminal record? The journey through incarceration and beyond has reshaped my understanding of justice, equity, and resilience.

The Silent Barriers: Reentry's Hidden Challenges

When I returned home, I believed my qualifications and network would ease my reentry. After all, I had a master's degree. I had a lengthy profession as a licensed practitioner for several decades. More importantly, I had a wonderful support system that had stood beside me every single day. I thought I had all the tools necessary for a seamless transition. I was wrong.

Instead, I encountered systemic roadblocks designed to keep people like me on the margins. Reentry is a labyrinth, filled with barriers that seem insurmountable. For me, the most glaring of these was the professional licensing system.

We all face barriers, but uniquely to justice-impacted individuals trying to work in the field of psychology and other highly regulated fields, some are nearly impossible to overcome. Not only it is difficult to get into accredited schools to receive the educational component required, but we also face the harsh reality that we are unable to get licensed in the very educational discipline we fought so hard to receive. Furthermore, we are often denied the opportunity of a job in the field because most positions require not only a license but a favorable criminal history check. And then there are the accrediting bodies, many of which will require all employees to be cleared on their background before granting accreditations to employers, making it difficult for employers to hire us, even if they are willing.

Therefore, the field of psychology, where I had spent decades building my career, effectively barred me from returning. Despite my education and experience, my criminal record disqualified me from the licenses I needed to practice. Licensing boards deemed me unfit, not because of incompetence but because of their inability to see beyond the stigma of incarceration. The cumulative effect of these rejections was devastating. Each "no" chipped away at my confidence, leaving me to wonder if the world would ever see me as more than my mistakes. The barriers went beyond employment. Housing, education, financial assistance, and even social reintegration felt like uphill battles.

The rejection wasn't just about a career; it was personal. I began to question my worth, my abilities, and my place in the world. Each rejection letter became a reminder of the societal stigma I carried. It was a painful realization that my past, no matter how unrelated to my professional competence, would dictate my future. The justice system may release you from physical confinement, but the invisible bars of stigma and systemic discrimination remain.

The Emotional Toll: Battling Self-Doubt and Imposter Syndrome

It is one thing to face external barriers; it is another to battle the internal demons they create.

After my incarceration, I found myself doubting most of my moves. The fear sometimes was paralyzing. And being rejected time and time again from securing a position in the very industry I had the best qualifications to be in, self-doubt started creeping in. Each rejection felt personal, leaving a scar and amplifying the voice inside me that whispered, "You're not good enough. You don't belong."

I began to question my skill set, my abilities, and my knowledge, and these feelings of self-doubt continued to grow with every rejection letter. Some call it imposter syndrome—which is defined by feelings of self-doubt and personal incompetence that persist despite an education, experience, and accomplishments.

Imposter syndrome became a constant companion. I questioned my abilities and my worth. I questioned whether I truly belonged in this new space, whether my voice had value in the fight for reform, even as I began to find success. The irony was painful: after spending years mastering my field, I now found myself a novice in the world of advocacy, trying to build credibility in a space I had never planned to enter.

The rejection from the very profession where my competence lay exacerbated that fear and confirmed my unfounded belief and feelings of inadequacy. It made me wonder, if not in my skill set, where do my strengths lie? If not in psychology, where then can I apply?

What saved me was the very experience of incarceration and the resilience I had built as a result of it. I began to reach out to several organizations that provided support for the justice-impacted community. There, I found a network of people who understood my journey. They reminded me that my experiences—both my triumphs and my struggles—were assets. Slowly, I began to see myself not as a failure, but as someone uniquely positioned to make an impact, not as an imposter but as a pioneer.

This is when I realized that my skills had not disappeared—they were still within me. The problem lies in society's inability to look beyond that one mistake, to give us an opportunity, to give us a second chance. Society is wired to reject anything that looks like our background because it poses a perceived risk.

We need to change this narrative; we need to show them that we come with vital skills that can improve many of the industries that we are being rejected from. This is why we tend to work twice as hard, not only to prove to them but most importantly to prove to ourselves that we still have value, that we still have worth, and that we are an integral part of their space. We need to remind ourselves that we belong.

I had found myself in a new industry—advocacy—no longer coming with the experience or knowledge that I had accumulated with my credentials through my professional career. But still having the transferable skills necessary for a fresh start in another industry, another field, another arena.

Finding My Voice: Building Bridges and Breaking Barriers

Ultimately, these impediments led me to take a different approach as to my career choices and expectations, forcing me to reinvent myself and my applications as a professional. Unable to return to my career in psychology, I turned to advocacy, not as a consolation prize but as a calling. I channeled my energy into advocacy, becoming a bridge between justice-impacted individuals and the opportunities they deserve.

Advocacy wasn't an entirely new path—it was an evolution. I used my clinical expertise to support others navigating reentry, offering not just guidance but empathy born from shared experience. My work allowed me to leverage my skills in a new way, connecting justice-impacted individuals with opportunities and resources. I became a speaker, a mentor, and a connector, ensuring that others didn't face the same isolation I had. In these roles, I found purpose and belonging.

I used my voice to shine a light on the systemic barriers that make reentry so challenging. I spoke at conferences, led policy initiatives, and collaborated with organizations that shared my vision for a more equitable justice system.

Advocacy became more than a job; it became a mission. That success, in many ways, strengthened my own inner self. Today, with each speech, each partnership, and each small victory, I grow stronger. I had discovered the power of lived experience. My time in prison had given me a perspective that no amount of academic training could replicate. I understood the fears, the doubts, and the resilience of justice-impacted individuals because I had lived them. This authenticity became my greatest strength, allowing me to connect with others in a way that was deeply personal and profoundly impactful.

I do this by putting into practice my professional background, my own knowledge, and my skill set, combining all of them with my personal experience with the legal system. But most importantly, I do so through the support that I have myself received from others. Having been able to connect with these and multiple other organizations that are doing amazing things for system-impacted individuals, and raising awareness of the issues that are faced during and after an incarceration, has been a life-saving experience for me.

Creating Opportunities: The Power of Community

If there's one lesson I've learned, it's this: when the system refuses to see your worth, you must create spaces that reflect your value. For me, that meant founding initiatives and forging partnerships that uplifted the justice-impacted community. It meant redefining what success looks like, not just for myself but for others walking the same path. This requires a network of support—people who see your potential, even when society does not.

For this very reason, I became involved with organizations that supported me and my reentry journey. I created an extensive network and support system of people who are like-minded and willing to give that second chance. In that network is where I found my calling for advocacy, by constantly being a bridge of collaboration and creating partnerships, with several organizations. I reached out to organizations like Unlock Higher Education (a program designed to support those interested in the pathway to higher education) and The Ladies of Hope Ministries (a program designed to assist those interested in a career pathway) whose goals align with my goals to help the justice-impacted community. They became my lifelines. They provided not only resources but also a sense of belonging. Through these networks, and many others, I found mentors, collaborators, and friends who reminded me that I was not alone. They have seen my skills and talents beyond the limitations I put on myself, due to my own insecurities.

These networks didn't just provide support; they reignited my belief in collective action and the power of community. They provided me a network, composed of like-minded community leaders, organizations, institutions, and advocates who are doing the work at the federal, state, and local levels in order to bring forth discussions of best practices in the reentry space to support individuals like me.

This opportunity simultaneously allowed me to embark in a successful reentry journey while continuing to voice my concerns about the need for criminal justice reform.

This sense of community has inspired me to pay it forward and do the same for others along their journey. As a mentor and speaker, I work to uplift others navigating reentry. I help them see their own potential and encourage them to rewrite the narratives society has imposed on us and our potential and worth in the workplace, thus increasing the spaces and places we can be successful in.

I am also a firm believer that by using our collective voices we can inspire change in those following in our footsteps. Together, we are educating those that keep the doors of opportunity shut and creating a movement—one that challenges the stigma of incarceration and redefines what it means to succeed after prison.

The Broader Impact: Advocacy as a Catalyst for Change

As I go on my journey, in the hopes of establishing a pathway to my career that represents once again that I am worthy of holding professional licenses, I look forward to being part of that impact that our stories bring. I know I am not an isolated case nor am I the first or the last to go through these barriers that have long been imposed by licensing boards and other entities.

The obstacles I faced are part of a larger problem. In fact, it is estimated that there are more than 44,000 barriers to reentry, restricting access not only to employment but also to essentials like education, housing, healthcare, and financial assistance—fundamentals for successful reintegration. These barriers are not just personal, they are systemic. They reflect a society that values punishment over rehabilitation and stigma over second chances. They are collateral consequences that continue way beyond the completion of a sentence, making it truly remarkable when anyone succeeds post-incarceration.

While these barriers are daunting, they are what fuel my resolve to become part of the solution. Through advocacy and collaboration, I am part of the many collective voices joined together in similar struggles, as we push forward in ultimately dismantling those barriers that impeded us from being recipients of a true second chance. Advocacy has shown me the importance of dismantling these systemic obstacles. Through it, I have come to see the broader implications of reentry. It is not just about helping individuals rebuild their lives; it is about dismantling the structures that make reintegration so difficult.

This work is not easy, but it is necessary. Every policy I help shape, every partnership I help build, is a step toward a more equitable society. It is a reminder that change is possible, even in the face of deeply entrenched systems. To me it is more than an individual success; it's about creating a society that values redemption and invests in second chances. It is about creating a world where everyone, regardless of their past, has the opportunity to rebuild, contribute, and thrive.

Today, I have come full circle with the organizations that supported me in my initial journey. Not only am I the Policy Team Lead for Unlock Higher Education, but I am also the Partnership Lead for The Ladies of Hope Ministries. I am also their Epic Ambassador for Florida. I am a mentor and a speaker for Prison to Professionals and a facilitator for the Ladies Empowerment Action Program. I am an Emerging Leaders and Leading with Conviction graduate, a Dream .org Justice Empathy fellow, and a Women Organizing for Justice & Opportunity member. I also sit on the Board of Directors for Evolution Reentry and Exchange for Change, two nonprofit organizations focused on assisting individuals during and after their incarceration.

I say all this not to elevate myself or to confirm my suspicions that I still suffer from a bit of imposter syndrome but to show that the journey to my career pathway took several years of growth and dedication, not only to find myself but to find where I felt I best fit in. Each role is a testament to the resilience of justice-impacted individuals and a reminder that our value isn't diminished by our pasts.

I also want to highlight that those places where I felt most accepted have a common thread. They are all in the criminal justice reform and advocacy arena. That is one space, one industry, because I chose to be that bridge maker in this particular industry. This should not be the case; we should be welcomed in all industries, as we have much to offer in diverse spaces. We come with a diverse skill set and plenty of experience.[1]

Conclusion: Reentry as Reinvention

For me, reentry has been a journey of reinvention. It has forced me to confront my fears, embrace my strengths, and find new ways to contribute, lead, and make an impact. It has taught me that resilience is not about avoiding failure but about rising each time you fall.

My story is just one among millions that reflect the potential for transformation when barriers are removed. With nearly 80 million Americans with a criminal record today, society has a financial obligation to begin to recognize the potential that individuals like me can bring to the workforce and has a moral obligation to begin to understand that we deserve a second chance. Therefore, I feel an obligation to take advantage of this opportunity to help change the narrative of how we are perceived by society today and hope to pave the way for others to reclaim their professional identities and contribute to society.

My hope is that in the future we are given a second chance as professionals. I hope to see that we are able, not only to be accepted in our fields of choice for educational advancement but to become licensed practitioners once again. Until then, I will voice my concerns, in the hopes that awareness will ultimately bring about that much-needed change. It is the new generations that drive the future of this system and the more awareness of the importance of these policies and how they affect the people they serve, the better understanding to create future policies that are fair, that are just, and that are equitable for all.

I recognize the positive impact that my skill set and support system have had in opening doors as I move forward toward my own restoration and second chance in life; I can only imagine how much harder it is for those individuals that never had those tools, never had the education. Those individuals never had a first chance. Because of that, this is not your typical story. I've had many of the resources they continue to lack. Yet, with approximately one in three Americans with a criminal record, this is your typical story. It's just that most stories have not been told.

Reentry isn't just about returning to society; it's about reclaiming your place in it. It is not the end of the story; it is the beginning of a new chapter, in telling your story. It's about transforming obstacles into opportunities and rewriting the narrative society imposes on you. It is a chance to redefine yourself, to turn those obstacles into opportunities, and to prove—to yourself and to the world—that you are more than your mistakes.

To those navigating reentry, I offer this: you are not alone. Your story matters, and your potential is limitless. Look beyond the limitations others place on you. If society can't see your worth, create opportunities that reflect your value. If a door closes, go knocking on the next one, and if you get a no, continue until you find your yes. You've already overcome far greater challenges than societal judgment. Your story isn't over—it's just beginning. Remember, reentry is not the end; it's the beginning of your reinvention.

Judith Negron, a Trump clemency recipient

Judith Negron with her husband on the night of her release from prison
Source: Photo by Judith Negron

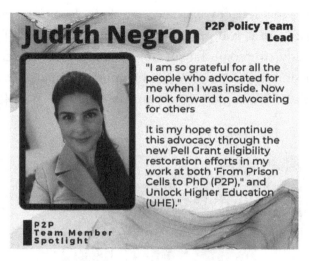

Judith Negron, P2P Policy Team Lead
Source: Photo by Judith Negron

Part II
Resilience

Chapter 5
Resilience and Perseverance Win

By Dr. Tommy Moore

> **Introduction to Dr. Tommy Moore's Chapter**
>
> *By Dr. Stanley Andrisse*
>
> Dr. Tommy Moore's journey exemplifies the transformative power of resilience, education, and mentorship. From overcoming immense challenges to earning a PhD and building a thriving business, Dr. Moore's story is one of determination and reinvention.
>
> I have had the privilege of witnessing Dr. Moore's growth firsthand. Through Prison to Professionals (P2P), he has used his experiences to inspire others, leveraging the support and platforms we provided to amplify his voice and elevate his story. Beyond his personal achievements, Dr. Moore's commitment to giving back through his business highlights his dedication to creating pathways for others navigating similar challenges.
>
> In this chapter, Dr. Moore delves into the unique barriers he faced, his unwavering resolve to overcome them, and the critical role education and mentorship played in reshaping his life. His accomplishments remind us of the profound impact of opportunity and community, and his work continues to inspire hope and transformation within the justice-impacted community.

Writing a chapter about resilience and perseverance never crossed my mind 24 years ago when a judge ordered me into custody of the Florida Department of Corrections on June 22, 2000, to serve a split 15-year sentence for a second-degree violent felony. After serving nine years and three months in four Florida prisons, I vividly remember the discharge officer sarcastically asking me if I planned to switch to white-collar crime since I spent much of my incarceration studying business and taking college courses. I told him, "I will earn a PhD in business and open my own company. Maybe one day you could come to work for me?"

Today, I hold a PhD in business administration (financial management) and own a licensed mental health facility in Florida employing 23 therapists and staff. I also teach entrepreneurship and business courses at a local state college and run a nonprofit organization that gives incarcerated individuals a second chance through education. I share these accomplishments not to boast but to show that second chances are possible—albeit with a price. That price includes resilience, perseverance, and a mindset that refuses to accept "no" as a final answer. When others told me, "You can't do it," I asked myself, "How can I do it?" In this chapter, I will highlight three pivotal points in my journey where resilience, perseverance, education, and mentorship enabled me to overcome unique challenges.

Childhood Struggles and Early Trauma

I was born in 1970 into a middle-class family in Orlando, Florida. My father worked as an electrical engineer for Lockheed Martin, and my mother was a public school teacher. I have one brother who is three years younger than me. My earliest memory was a woman from my mom's Methodist church telling me, "God will use you in mighty ways when you grow up." At the time, this seemed far from the truth.

Around age 10, my family moved to Germany for my father's defense project. Unable to live on the military base, I faced culture shock and struggled to adapt. During this time, a teenage girl seduced me, and when I couldn't perform, the resulting bullying left deep scars. I adopted survival coping mechanisms like seeking performance-based acceptance and trying to appear important, which would shape my decisions for years to come.

When we returned to the United States, I was 12 years old. A 20-year-old neighbor molested me, and I felt ashamed, dirty, and confused. Afraid he might target my younger brother, I allowed the abuse to continue. This secret led to resentment and anger, which I directed at my brother and everyone around me. I turned to drugs and alcohol to numb my feelings, spiraling out of control by age 15. Desperate to intervene, my father took me to a tough-love rehab program called "Scared Straight." He set a boundary when I escaped: I could return home only after completing the program. After escaping again, I ended up living on the streets of Orlando, hopeless and defeated.

Turning Points: Faith and Resilience

One night, after sleeping behind a dumpster, covered in bug bites, I wandered into Orlando Christian Center, led by Pastor Benny Hinn. God met me at the door, and Benny took me in. He sent me to a Christian program called "Loving Hands," where I immersed myself in scripture and began to heal. Benny even arranged for me to attend Oral Roberts University. However, I hadn't addressed my past traumas, and without accountability, I drifted away from faith when I began living inconsistently with its principles.

By the late 1990s, I was living recklessly. I drank daily, used drugs, and sought validation from others—even as my financial situation deteriorated. I stopped attending church and would go to a bar every night with the guys for a few drinks. I got my first DUI in 1995, and I remember feeling like my career was over, and I was determined to quit. I promised I would only drink at home, and I would never drink and drive again. And I didn't for about a month. My reckless behavior was about fun, and I convinced myself I wasn't hurting anyone. The turning point came in 1999 when a tragic car accident caused by my intoxicated driving claimed a life. The grief and guilt drove me to my lowest point. I remember my mom walking into my room and saying, "The passenger didn't make it." I remember falling to my knees and yelling at God. NOOOOOO!!! NOOOO! That morning was the lowest point of my life.

I vividly remember looking at the pull-up bar out in the backyard and tying a rope in a knot, trying to build up the courage to end my life. Because of this tragic event, the judge sentenced me to 11 years in prison, four years' probation, loss of my driver's license, and restitution. So I entered the Florida prison system at 29 years old with a six-month-old son, convinced I would never make it out alive, but God had other plans.

I began the arduous work of rebuilding myself. I rededicated my life to Christ, attended Alcoholics Anonymous, and started working through the 12 Steps. Prison taught me that freedom is a spiritual state, not merely a physical one. I found purpose in mentoring others, taking business courses, and preparing for life beyond incarceration. I realized I could still be free despite being behind a razor wire. When the guards would come by and clang my bunk, yelling "Get up, Convict" and "Let's go, Scumbag," I would wash my face while looking in the scratched-up plastic mirror and say quietly to myself, I'm not a convict, I'm not a scumbag, I'm a child of the king, and I would walk to the recreation field with a mindset of royalty. People would come to me and ask how I had hope in such a harsh environment. Did I even feel the suffocating oppression that seemed to occupy the air constantly? That always allowed me to witness and confirm that my circumstances did not define me. Although I did not know how it would work out, I knew God was working things out for my good.

I made some amends with my brother, who would come on annual visits. He had channeled his life toward positive things and had earned his way to the executive director of Chicago Trade on the Chicago Board of Options Exchange. One day, I opened mail from him. He agreed to pay for college business classes, one class a year, beginning immediately. So, I began taking college business courses through Ohio University's College for the Incarcerated Program (CIP). I fell in love with the topic of business. I started asking my dad to invest some of my commissary money, instructing him where I wanted it. God worked on my life by giving me hope in a dark valley. God gave me favor with guards and inmates, and I began learning A/C work, electrical work, and motor pool work. It wasn't desirable, but it beat the mow squad. I don't want to glamorize prison; it sucked, and it was often very volatile and highly frightening. It was hard to stay sober with the abundant drug supply and the pain of watching my son grow up in pictures. I had two major surgeries while incarcerated and almost died once when I did not seek medical attention, which stemmed from extreme dehydration. But I always felt that if it was my turn to go home, I was going to a better place.

Education as a Catalyst for Change

Released in 2009, I faced the challenge of reintegration. I attended church regularly, unsuccessfully looked for work, and honestly had a hard time reintegrating into society. I applied to my local community college, but the administrator said I would not be admitted.

I remember coming home triggered by rejection, insufficiency, and unworthiness. But this time, I called my mentor, asked for prayer, and trusted God. The next day, the same enrollment advisor who gave me the admission denial news called me and said, "Mr. Moore, I have worked here for over 20 years, and this doesn't happen, but they will give you one semester on probation." That was all I needed. I took that offer in 2009 and encountered my first unique challenge since serving almost a decade in prison. I had no driver's license, and the school was 10 miles from home. I knew the power of education, so I resiliently pedaled my bike 10 miles a day to attend classes. Envision a middle-aged man—I went into prison at 29 years old and exited at 39 years old—riding his bike in the middle of Florida summer to the local community college. One afternoon, I remember young girls between 18 and 20 years old telling me I should exercise after class because I came into school "stinking." I laughed with them and said, "You're probably right. I should consider exercising after class." They did not know that it was my only way to arrive if I wanted my education.

In 2011, I earned my associate in arts degree and automatically had the right to enter the University of Central Florida in Orlando through a direct connect program contract that the two institutions had entered into. The University of Florida mandated I be placed on probation since I would attend on campus. The administration was not glad I had the same automatic enrollment privileges as the other students who graduated with an associate in arts degree from the community college. My second unique challenge was getting there without a driver's license. Fortunately, there was an option, but it would require resilience, perseverance, and a lot of patience. I had the option of public transportation. I rode a city bus five hours a day, two-and-a-half hours each way, five days a week for two years, from 2011 to 2013. In that time I earned, with honors, my bachelor of science in business administration (finance) degree.

I remember nearing the end of my undergraduate tenure at UCF and wanting to come off probation before graduating. I had amassed more than 30 letters of recommendation, had earned the "President's List" multiple semesters, and even been inducted into the elite Phi Kappa Phi honor society. I was granted a hearing and remember entering the interview with high hopes. If anyone had shown that change could happen, I had the tangible evidence to present to the board. I remember one doctor on the panel speaking out. He said, "I work with addicts and alcoholics every day, and you all try to manipulate us for favorable outcomes. If I have my way, you will not come off probation as long as you're on this campus." I remember the chairman of the interview saying, "What do you have to say to that, Mr. Moore?" I replied, "God grant me the serenity to accept the things I cannot change, courage to change the things I can, and wisdom to know the difference. I can't change whether or not you let me off probation, but I can continue earning straight As in my next two colleges in pursuit of my PhD." Everyone at the table smiled, and I thought I was in a good position. They asked me to exit the room while they deliberated and brought me back in. The chairman then told me I would not come off probation while I was at the university. No one promised me it would be easy, but I knew it would be worth it if I did my part. I did just what I said I would, and in 2015, I earned my master's in business administration (finance) degree from the Florida Institute of Technology. On June 10, 2020, in the heart of the coronavirus pandemic, I defended my dissertation and earned my PhD in business administration (financial management) from Northcentral University.

Entrepreneurship and Giving Back

Despite my qualifications, finding employment as a felon was nearly impossible. Everywhere I went, employers wanted to know if I had a felony. I remember my probation officer telling me if I did not produce a W2 in the next week, he would be required to send me back to prison. Facing the threat of returning to prison due to unemployment, I started a real estate investment business with my father. Applying the principles I learned in school, we grew and sold the company in 2014. The proceeds from the sale allowed my dad to retire for the rest of his life and gave me about three years of living expenses. I began giving back to my community and using my business education to help with a recovery program at my local church. We started with two groups and about 12 people. In a few years, we had grown to 12 groups and more than 300 people in attendance. The church committee said, "We must hire Tommy on staff because he is on our campus too often to justify volunteering." So, I began getting paid as a recovery leader and kept my eyes open for the next opportunity.

I had always dreamed of authoring a book after my prison release titled *From Prison to PhD*, and so I began embarking on that journey. I wanted to know if anyone had the right to that title. A simple Google search connected me with Dr. Stanley Andrisse, who would change my life trajectory. He had already authored a book and was an accomplished professor. He had just founded a reentry program called Prison to Professionals in Baltimore, and I knew I had to try to connect with him. I got the nerve to write him an email and ask if he would be willing to mentor me since he had already accomplished what I desired. He said he would, but I must attend his program first. He emphasized that he invested in potential and wanted to see if I was genuine in my effort to succeed. I did not graduate from that first cohort of the P2P Scholars program. I entered and left before completing cohort 8, but I returned and graduated with cohort 11. Dr. Andrisse remained true to his word and began giving me opportunities to partner with P2P, and he gave me a platform to use my voice in second-chance advocacy.

Since then, I have dedicated my life to helping others. In December 2017, my best friend and I opened Priority One Coaching, Counseling & Consulting for the primary purpose of helping people in our community. We now have 23 licensed mental health marriage and family therapists who practice in our two locations near Orlando and Tampa, Florida. I have had the honor of helping hundreds of people work through deep-rooted issues and watching them flourish and become the best version of themselves. I now have more than 24 years of uninterrupted sobriety from drinking alcohol, with more years of being sober than I have with drinking. I own my home, and God has bought me a beautiful wife, daughter, and mother-in-law. My wife and I have been married for more than eight years now. She loves me for me and holds me accountable to be the God-fearing husband, father, and man I claim to be. My relationship with my son has thrived in authenticity and has never been better. I teach business classes at my local community college as an adjunct professor. I also work for a nonprofit in Nebraska focused on helping people successfully reintegrate into society.

Relationship Restoration

My relationship with my parents has grown exponentially. People used to ask me, "Why are you majoring in finance? Florida will not give you a financial advisor license, and no one will hire an ex-felon to manage their money." I had no good answer. I didn't know why God led me to this field. Then, in September 2017, in the second year of my doctorate, my dad asked me to review my parents' retirement portfolio. I uncovered that their life savings remained in high-commissioned financial products that were way too risky for their age tolerance. God gave me the honor of helping them get away from the insurance sales associates' advisors and into a well-diversified portfolio in a reputable financial firm. I realized that going to school for finance was never about managing a lot of money in corporate America. God had used finance strictly as a medium to reconcile a relationship between a father and son. I'll never forget the day my dad told me he believed I was on his team again.

A Message of Hope

To anyone feeling hopeless, I want to emphasize that your past does not define your future. Resilience, education, and mentorship can transform even the most challenging circumstances. The journey won't be easy, but it will be worth it. Stay committed to doing the next right thing, even when no one is watching, and extend grace to yourself as you grow. Today, I am living proof that second chances are real, and God continues to work all things together for good. I have gone from prison to PhD and won through resilience, education, and mentorship. Thank you, Dr. Andrisse, for believing in me.

From prison to PhD, resilience has been my guide—and it can be yours, too.

Old me and Prison to PhD me

Chapter 6

Journey to Liberating the Institutionalized Mind

By Desiree Riley

Introduction to Desiree's Chapter

By Dr. Stanley Andrisse

"Sis, we can't keep going on like this. It's either jail or worse." Desiree's own voice echoed in her mind, a warning she could no longer ignore. She sat on the edge of her leather couch—one of the few possessions that hinted at stability, though the reality beneath it was anything but. The weight of poverty wasn't just financial; it was emotional, mental, and relentless. It seeped into every decision, every sleepless night, every desperate calculation of what bill could wait another week. The world pressed down on her shoulders as she met the gaze of the small, innocent face looking up at her. Her son was everything—her purpose, her reason to keep pushing. But how do you fight a system designed for you to fail? How do you outrun the exhaustion of poverty when every path forward is laced with barriers meant to keep you exactly where you are?

Desiree's journey is one of perseverance in the face of systemic injustice. Poverty, often described as the invisible cage,

(continued)

(continued)

traps millions in a cycle that is difficult to escape. Economic hardship doesn't just challenge survival; it increases the likelihood of engaging in illegal activities as a means to an end. Studies show that low-income individuals are disproportionately incarcerated, largely because survival often necessitates decisions that wealthier individuals are never forced to consider.

The so-called "War on Drugs" further stacked the deck against people like Desiree. Harsh sentencing laws for nonviolent drug offenses tore families apart and filled prisons with individuals from marginalized communities. According to the Brennan Center for Justice, these policies have contributed to the exponential growth of mass incarceration since the 1980s, disproportionately affecting women of color like Desiree.

For Desiree, the criminalization of poverty added another layer of oppression. She had been penalized for things others took for granted: unpaid fines, the inability to post bail, and moments of desperation that turned into criminal charges. The system didn't care about her story or the children depending on her—it only cared about punishment.

But Desiree refused to let the system write her narrative. She didn't just break the chains of her own circumstances; she began forging pathways for others. Her organization, The MasterMind Cooperative, is now a beacon of hope for justice-impacted individuals. Through her work, she has amplified the voices of others facing the same struggles she endured. And through her YouTube channel, Revolutionary Travel Family,[1] she has shown the world how love and determination can help a family thrive and explore together.

Desiree credits her transformative journey in part to her involvement with Prison to Professionals (P2P). "Dr. Stanley Andrisse invited me to this honorable opportunity, and it expanded my

> mind to a new world of possibilities," she says with a smile that now carries the light of hope. For Desiree, P2P wasn't just an organization; it was a family that showed her how to rewrite her story.
>
> This chapter is a celebration of Desiree's resilience, a reminder of the systemic barriers that exist, and a call to action to dismantle them. Her story demonstrates that, while poverty, injustice, and systemic racism may seek to hold individuals down, the power of hope, community, and education can create pathways to liberation.
>
> Desiree is proof that it is never too late to do good—"Li pa janm twò ta pou fè byen."

Breaking free from the chains of incarceration is more than just a physical release; it's a profound mental and emotional journey. Nelson Mandela once said, "The greatest glory in living lies not in never falling, but in rising every time we fall." This resonates deeply with the theme of this work: liberating the institutionalized mind. In a world that often seeks to define people by their past mistakes, reclaiming one's life requires an unwavering commitment to personal growth, resilience, and self-transformation.

This journey is not just about overcoming the physical barriers of incarceration but also about breaking free from the mental and emotional chains that continue to bind individuals even after their release. Personal liberation from both mental and physical imprisonment is crucial for formerly incarcerated individuals as we navigate the path to reclaiming our future and redefining our identity.

My journey from confinement to freedom is a testament to the human spirit's ability to rise above circumstances and redefine destiny. My name is Desiree Riley, but many people call me Dezi. I am the founder of The MasterMind Cooperative (TMC), a personal development nonprofit that I wish was available to me at various stages of my life. As a mother once facing 6–30 years in prison, I believe it's my duty to build a better world for the future. The following text shares some concepts and background details from my autobiographical work, *Felony to Freedom*.

This chapter delves into one such journey—my journey—from the depths of despair and institutionalization to the heights of personal and mental liberation. It aims to illustrate the transformative power of resilience, personal growth, and self-discovery, offering hope and guidance to those who seek to overcome their past and reclaim their future.

To fully appreciate the depth of my transformation, it's important to understand the major milestones in my journey: from the traumatic incident in Chicago that led to my arrest, through the dehumanizing process of incarceration, to the profound internal changes that shaped my outlook on life. Each of these experiences played a crucial role in my development and led to the creation of TMC, with steadfast dedication to helping others discover their individual paths to freedom.

Desiree book signing, c. 2024

The Turning Point

I'll always remember that cold winter morning in 2012 …

I'd just left Marshall's in a small strip mall outside Chicago, Illinois. My son and I stayed in a shabby inn after a long drive from Detroit, Michigan. It was the week Whitney Houston passed. I decided to buy him a few long-sleeve button-up shirts for Sunday school for a church we had recently joined in Columbus, Ohio. We left the store with a couple of small bags and about $42 in change.

As expected, my brand-new Toyota Corolla was parked precisely where I had left it. Relieved that I could finally be done with the uncertain mission I was on, we hopped in and proceeded carefully down the road. Beanie Siegel wrote, "I can feel it in the air," and I definitely could. Things didn't feel right since the moment I woke up, but I believed we needed money, so the job had to get done.

About a mile down the road, a nondescript dark vehicle pulled behind me and turned on interior police lights. My heart sank, and a wave of panic washed over me. "This can't be happening," I thought, my mind racing through a thousand scenarios. The fear of what was about to happen was paralyzing. My son was in the backseat, completely unaware of the gravity of the situation. As I pulled over, I felt a profound sense of regret and desperation. How did I let it come to this?

The officers approached my car, and as the reality of my situation began to set in, I fought back the tears welling up in my eyes. My thoughts were a chaotic mess of fear, guilt, and sorrow. "What will happen to my son? Will I ever see him again?"

The weight of my choices crushed me, and in that moment, I began to reflect on every decision that had led me here. The reality of my choices, the desperation that had driven me to take such risks, all played out in my mind like a tragic movie. I prayed that the contents were discreetly stored in my vehicle and there would be no immediately visible evidence.

When they popped the trunk, the heavy fragrance of densely packed marijuana was impossible to miss. Zero effort was spent trying to hide anything—pounds and pounds of it. One officer politely let me know that I wouldn't see my son again until he was my age. I prayed I could get this all sorted out and return home before my mother ever realized I'd been arrested. The following day, I was notified that I'd be facing 6–30 years in prison on a Class X Felony charge.

Lessons Learned

I recently read that the average adult faces about 35,000 decision-making moments each day (Reill, 2023). The choices that led me to that moment in 2012 were a mix of desperation and misguided hope. Reflecting on my arrest, I began to understand how each small decision had built up to this pivotal point in my life. The pressure to provide for my family, the fear of failure, and the allure of a quick solution had clouded my judgment.

As we sat in the back of a large black SUV that arrived shortly after I was pulled over, I was reminded that every choice has a consequence. This understanding became a cornerstone of my personal philosophy. I began to see the importance of making decisions that align with my values and long-term goals. This realization was the first step in my journey toward personal growth and transformation.

I made a choice out of desperation that could have ruined my life and left my son without his mother. Over the years since that day, I've learned to allow my choices to be guided by future-forward thinking. How would I prefer to spend the next 6–30 years? Will this choice lead me there? Each of my choices is still not always ideal. I often wrestle with an addiction to junk food and could choose to get in more steps daily. Our reality reflects our choices, as the summation of our decisions builds the habits that make up our daily lives.

It's the choices we make that shape who we become and how we spend this time we call life. Choices determine not only how we live but also how we die. Choices on who we make connections with, what we consume, and how we spend our time. Each decision impacts our quality of life and those we interact with, whether positively, negatively, or neutrally. Though not much is neutral. Every choice guides our journey as we navigate as sovereign beings.

Breaking the Cycle of Financial Trauma

My time in jail taught me invaluable lessons about resilience, patience, and the power of a positive mindset. But before I could fully embrace those lessons, I had to confront a deeper truth—one that had shaped so many of my past decisions: financial trauma had been a constant force in my life, dictating my choices in ways I didn't always recognize.

Growing up with limited resources meant survival often took precedence over stability. The pressure of unpaid bills, the fear of not having enough to feed my children, and the desperation that comes with never feeling financially secure led me to make choices I might not have considered under different circumstances. It wasn't just about money; it was about the mental toll of scarcity, the stress of constantly trying to stay afloat, and the belief that opportunities weren't meant for people like me. Even after incarceration, financial instability remained a barrier, making it difficult to access housing, employment, and a fresh start. The system wasn't built for redemption—it was designed to keep people like me stuck.

Research shows that financial trauma, often exacerbated by economic hardship and limited opportunities, traps individuals in a constant state of stress and survival mode. Financial insecurity is a significant driver of criminal behavior, as people sometimes resort to illegal activities out of sheer desperation to meet basic needs

(Gålnander, 2022; Guan, 2022). This cycle is reinforced by systemic inequities, including restricted access to legitimate financial opportunities, inadequate support systems, and a justice system that punishes poverty rather than addressing its root causes. I didn't need to read studies to know this—I had lived it.

Breaking this cycle requires more than just resilience; it requires access to real solutions—financial literacy, mental health support, and stable employment opportunities. These are the guiding principles behind Project Phoenix, the newest initiative at The MasterMind Cooperative designed to support at-risk young adults. Launched in Philadelphia, Project Phoenix aims to address financial trauma head-on, equipping participants with the tools they need to heal, build economic stability, and create a future beyond survival. Because I know firsthand that when people have the right resources, they don't just survive—they transform their lives.

Rebuilding After Incarceration

Upon my release, I knew that I couldn't navigate this path alone. I needed a support system that believed in my potential and would help me stay on track. Family, friends, and mentors played a crucial role in my recovery and growth. One of the most important suggestions I would make to another person is to never decide solely based on desperation if possible. We all know that sometimes life just happens, and we find ourselves stuck between a rock and a hard place. Many times, we and our loved ones also have to live with the inevitable consequences.

My life has taken many wild twists and turns. From my early days of shoplifting to facing a lengthy prison sentence, my journey has been marked by learning and transformation. I never imagined being in the fortunate situation I am in now. While I was in middle school in Philly, I began stealing from stores. I thought I was saving money or taking things I "couldn't afford" from people who had a lot of money. Luckily, this period in my life didn't last long. Soon, I started losing things I cherished. I chose to believe that if I stopped stealing, I could keep what I earned and really wanted. This way of thinking continues to work out for me.

When I relocated to Columbus, Ohio, to live with my paternal grandmother Alice Whaley at age 15, I began making new, and more wholesome, friends. I ended up enjoying school tremendously and even decided to go to college. Shortly after high school, I traveled to Louisiana for the first time and enrolled in Grambling State University. During the era of Hurricane Katrina, I faced the most stressful relationship I could have imagined (at that time). After a child, years of cohabitation, and a failed engagement, I decided to wait for what was suitable for me while developing myself into a more suitable partner.

Personal Growth and Transformation

Growth and transformation doesn't happen overnight. It continues to be a gradual process of self-discovery, learning, and adapting. Each day presented new challenges, but also new opportunities for growth. I learned to embrace my journey and use my experiences as fuel for my mission to help others.

I made many poor decisions based on my desire to speed to the "next level" in life. Everything felt like a competition due to unaddressed trauma and conflicts of self-worth because I had been disregarded so many times since I was a young child. The rise of social media only exacerbated the issue—I had to win! Whether it was to win a terrible mate, win a job I would soon hate, or win a title I didn't really want—I just had to win. I've been grateful to learn, in recent years, that I am only competing with myself to become the best version of myself. I am honoring my path, lessons, and connections, and I feel extremely blessed that I no longer want things that are not for me.

We must remember that everyone we read about, see online, or watch on television is only human. These people have made choices or have been surrounded by others who made choices that led them to where we discovered them. The life we desire is just a responsible set of committed choices away. No one is any better than we are; some are just more dedicated to their goals. There is no reason to want their lives or idolize other humans.

Healing and Self-Reflection

Healthy minds make healthy choices. Too often, we self-medicate from the pain we still feel and the memories of neglect using addictive substances or behaviors like food, drugs, sex, gambling, productivity, social media, or being overly busy. These are coping mechanisms to deal with those feelings, the stress that comes after the trauma, and the trauma that comes because of the stress. While my childhood wasn't as bad as many I know about, many of my behaviors in relationships and parenting directly correspond with interactions I experienced in early life.

Healthy minds make healthy choices
Source: Photo by Desiree J. Riley

Often, we disregard our issues because we believe they're not as deep as others' or as bad. We compare them and validate them against the level of tragedy others have faced. When we do that, we don't give ourselves time to properly heal and adjust to the truth of what we have experienced and/or are still experiencing. Our experiences are valid, and they do matter. They shape who we are and the person we will become. They also shape the kind of people we will raise; the people we are currently raising. To self-heal, we must acknowledge all these things. It causes us to dig deep and lift scabs, uncovering Band-Aids and wounds that haven't healed but may have just been concealed.

Healing is crucial because without it, old wounds remain open. They will only fester over time when covered and neglected, much like a gunshot wound hidden behind a sleeve. The sooner painful and damaging issues are addressed, cleansed, treated, and healed, the better our lives will be. Making self-healing a habit can be one of the most beneficial skills any human can develop. We can take these practices and help heal others or pay the information forward, sharing steps that helped us most effectively. When old injuries leave scars, the new skin is thicker and stronger.

Embracing Resilience

I intentionally built an inner circle that valued loyalty because my aversion to betrayal was serious. My circle became almost nonexistent, limited to my immediate family, some cousins, and a few friends I saw occasionally. I preferred it this way. Even though I valued building community, it was hard to let people get close when many valued only what I could do for them.

It was refreshing when I could connect with people who genuinely liked who I was. They valued my contributions to any situation, and those feelings were reciprocated in mutually beneficial relationships. I highly prize my current connections and also enjoy maintaining a very tight circle (at this time).

While in jail awaiting my fate, I decided to fast and read the Bible with a couple of new friends. We started at Matthew and concluded with Mark. During those three days, I became aware of the pattern of those who had court dates nearby. The day before, they would seem very positive and behave like newly reformed people. Then, when they came back with a continuance (which happened most often) or worse news, they would return angrier or more defeated than when they first arrived. Few of the lessons of the situation were being learned or recognized. I clearly noticed myself changing into a different and more aggressive person. Through the realization and acceptance of the lesson that I would not get through this situation until I recognized what character flaws landed me there, I believe I was blessed with early release. It is our responsibility to learn and graduate or surrender to forces that will have us repeat the same lessons over and over.

Moving Forward

Lessons are life's teaching tools. Tests are not passed until the lessons are learned. I'm reminded of this often, and I'm grateful to have the understanding and faith. I've watched cycles repeat day after day, year after year, and lessons still fail to be learned. I've learned that everyone must learn their own lessons in their own time. Proper guidance and examples can point us in the right direction, but we cannot rush others to embrace their lessons. I personally prefer to learn my lessons as quickly as possible in order to graduate to each new level while there is still vitality and breath in my body. Through this, my children can learn from my lessons, and we can offer worthy contributions to human evolution.

Sovereignty and personal freedom begin with controlling our thoughts or carefully crafting and curating the content that influences our thoughts. Some of us might have to delete half of our "friends" or remove social media altogether. Do we want to be accepted, or do we want to control our lives?

When we begin to have thoughts that are not in alignment with the future we want, we can gently redirect our thoughts to more beneficial ones, intentionally feed ourselves more beneficial content, and slowly eliminate nonbeneficial content, just like someone going on a diet. Self-discipline does not have to be painful. Gradual changes are most beneficial and sustainable, meaning they are much more likely to last for your entire life.

Encouragement and Advice

Allow mistakes and corrections to guide us toward our ultimate purpose. Keep failing until you succeed.

There is this meme where a man is digging in search of diamonds. After digging for years, he decides to quit and turn around for home. Then another man shows up and resumes the previous man's digging. After a few more feet, he discovers a massive diamond mine. Simply put, never quit progressing.

With the right mindset and intention synced with consistency, things will always work out eventually. Do not doubt yourself or your purpose. Keep going until you make it, and then keep going some more. True purpose lasts a lifetime. We should never stop learning and growing. Failure makes success feel so much better. How can anyone truly appreciate blissfulness if they have never experienced despair? Imagine digging for a beautiful diamond for years and quitting just inches before you reach it. Would it be worse to live a life full of pursuing your passion rather than a "safe" life where you quit early due to fear and self-doubt? I would prefer to die without those types of regret.

I appreciate the people I have met over the past decade, from all around the world. As someone without siblings, the advice and guidance from these entrepreneurs and open-minded people have sustained me. They are messages of self-confidence and empowerment, or how not to externalize my confidence and try to be like anyone else, and that I can only be myself.

I get hard on myself a lot, as if I don't know this is a marathon, as if I expected to have everything together overnight. This journey is a lifelong process. Going back to health as an example, my goals are more based on longevity, feeling good, and being an active parent than trying to get a perfect body. Again, I'm reminded not to compare myself to anyone else.

We all lose sometimes. I always call for the best while preparing for the worst. Like death, I don't see loss as an end. I know things will bounce back better in due time. That belief is my safety net. Advanced mental preparation virtually eliminates devastation by disappointment. This way, you are not naive to the flexural motion of life and seldom caught by surprise. This practice has not attracted more misfortune to my life overall, but it has strengthened my emotional resilience.

Practical Tips for Success

When we begin to rush ourselves, chances are we're falling into traps of comparison. Focus on your journey. You're the only one on your path, no matter how long it takes. When tuned into your own life, no one can possibly play your role; what's for you is yours alone.

To get on the right vibrations, we must switch frequencies. We must move ourselves mentally, spiritually, and maybe even physically to align with our visions. It's not possible to have the life you want by doing what you've always done or taking advice from people who have never made it happen. We must remove the chains of others' opinions and doubts of ourselves.

Writing taught me to share more openly. It required vulnerability and trust and became a healing journey for me. I knew that paranoia wasn't healthy, and I knew that isolation wasn't always beneficial. I wanted to grow and improve on my weaknesses, personal limitations, and flaws. I want my children to grow up feeling free to share their trust and love for others, but I believe that a healthy balance and awareness of the world are equally important.

Ongoing Journey and Future Vision

I turn 39 this year (2025), so I know I don't have all the answers. However, I want to share what I've gathered so far in this journey. If it impacts just one person on this planet, I feel like it's done its job. Even if it only impacts somebody 300 years from now or 2000 years from now, I've done my job. I feel like it was worth it.

I'm grateful for those who read this today and who will read it tomorrow. I'm thankful for those who will share this. I'm grateful for those who embark on their journey of self-healing through reading our words. I'm thankful for all of you for being alive, being resilient, and choosing to consume the content you believe will add value to your life. If you haven't heard it enough, I am proud of you. Too often, we don't hear those words of encouragement. It's important to let other people know that you're proud of them, especially when they're trying to do the right thing for themselves.

In the aftermath of reclaiming my life from the shadows of incarceration, the journey didn't end; it evolved. The process of transformation is perpetual, fueled by new challenges, growth, and the drive to make a lasting impact. This continuation of my journey delves into the ongoing pursuit of freedom, personal development, and the relentless effort to uplift others on similar paths as life has continued to unfold in unexpected and rewarding ways.

I've traveled around the world and had multiple home births both assisted and unassisted. As a mother of five now (John, Freedom, Love, Noble, and Glory), ranging from 18 years to 10 months, three of whom are dual citizens, the dynamics of my life are constantly shifting. My eldest child, John, has embarked on his own journey of service and growth through FEMA and AmeriCorps before heading to college, a testament to the values of hard work and community service that I strive to instill in all my children.

The MasterMind Coop is flourishing beyond what I originally imagined. What started as a vision to support personal development and community upliftment has now become a beacon of hope and transformation for many. Through programs, workshops, and collaborative efforts, we have empowered numerous individuals to break free from their own chains, whether literal or metaphorical, and embrace their true potential.

Here are some gems I have collected along my journey:

- Dare to dream and take the first step toward realizing your aspirations. Prepare and organize yourself, ensuring a solid foundation for your journey. Above all, love yourself first; self-love is the cornerstone of all success.
- Practice makes perfect. Mastery takes time and experience, and while this may vary depending on natural aptitude and access to resources, practice is essential. Your goal may not be perfection, but as your mind and body adjust to new habits, improvements will come naturally.
- Focus on a product, service, or trade you're passionate about. Make it a family affair, involving your loved ones in your endeavors. Establish a productivity schedule to manage your time effectively. Collaborate with like-minded individuals and always think for yourself.

- Create daily rituals that support your goals and don't absorb external negativity. Always give back to your community and remember to breathe deeply, expanding your chest and taking in the world around you.
- Share your story using your authentic voice and meditate on your goals regularly. Build or join a support group and be your own hype person. Encourage yourself and find creative ways to build brand loyalty. Be patient with your progress and take breaks when needed. Recognize when it's time to evolve and keep evolving.
- Don't be intimidated by big ideas and show love to others. Be a good example and live a life you love. Offer nothing but your best, understanding that some sacrifice is necessary. You don't need to have all the answers; be open to new solutions and don't be too proud to accept help. Walk in your truth and avoid doing things solely for fame. Stay in your lane, make time for rest and relaxation, and strive to become the very best version of yourself.
- Remember you're unique. Make time for your family and understand that your work is never finished. Take care of yourself and don't try to do everything at once. It's okay to keep some ideas in your mind for now. Things will get easier, and your daily routine will soon become second nature.
- Don't be afraid to shine bright or to call meetings with influential people. Don't fear rejection or any form of failure as experiencing fear is natural. However, living in a state of fear can paralyze you. Embrace fear but don't let it control you.
- Conduct regular ego checks and ensure your business isn't running you. Expect the unexpected and brace yourself for challenges. Be yourself and remember to socialize without feeling the need to assimilate. Know your worth and invest in yourself and wellness is key. Adopt favorable habits and drop unfavorable ones, cultivating your character.

- Don't let corrupt individuals dim your light. Stand out so you don't have to fit in and know it's okay to get it wrong sometimes. Don't be too proud to admit when you're wrong. Have fun and serve humanity, always protecting Mother Earth. Become stronger than your temptations and understand that being ordinary won't earn you bonus points. Eliminate debt quickly and heed wise counsel. Clearly recognize a mentor from a hater.

- Procrastination leads to failure, but don't be discouraged by failure. Take responsibility for your problems and don't take your frustrations out on your loved ones. Internalize your lessons and stay grounded, being reasonable with yourself. Your family is the priority.

- Practice sound therapy and write down your thoughts on pen and paper. Go with your gut and don't be afraid to be called a dreamer. Analyze your own toxic behaviors and reprogram your mind. Be loyal, especially to yourself, and don't let the curse of normality hold you back. Identify your children's passions and talents early and never listen to haters. Avoid subscribing to the opinions of losers.

- Implement small operational changes (SOCs) and appreciate your support system. Remember you are powerful, capable, and independent. You are worthy of success, happiness, and abundance. You have the power to achieve your dreams and goals, and you are fearless and unapologetically yourself. You are a leader and an innovator, surrounded by supportive and empowering people. You are confident in your abilities and decisions, resilient in the face of challenges, and grateful for your blessings, always attracting more.

- You are a force to be reckoned with, unstoppable, and worthy of love, respect, and happiness. You are strong, resilient, and capable of achieving anything you set your mind to. You embrace your unique culture and heritage and are not defined by your race, physical/mental abilities, or gender. You are deserving of self-care and take the time to nurture your mind, body, and spirit. You are not perfect, and that is okay. You are learning to love yourself exactly as you are. You are a powerful person making a positive impact on the world. You are enough, loved, and truly yourself.

- Cultivate a more positive mindset by practicing gratitude and mindfulness daily, leading to increased overall well-being and resilience. Start your days with mindfulness meditation and gratitude journaling. Reflect on positive experiences, practice deep breathing, and engage in activities that bring joy. Build positive connections with loved ones, visualize success, and take breaks to enjoy nature. Practice positive self-talk, appreciate small moments, and keep evolving toward your goals.

Final Thoughts

As I look toward the future, I am filled with a sense of purpose and gratitude. The journey to liberate my institutionalized mind is ongoing, a continuous process of growth, learning, and impact. With each step forward, I am reminded that the human spirit's capacity to rise above circumstances is boundless. This is a testament to the enduring strength and potential within us all. While we still have breath in our bodies, we can still make small incremental decisions that will lead us in the direction that we want to follow.

Healing is a continuous process, not just a final destination. From the moment of my arrest, through the despair of incarceration, to the joy of finding my purpose, healing played an integral role in my journey. Reflecting on my choices and their consequences was painful but necessary. It allowed me to confront my past, accept my mistakes, and move forward with a clearer vision for my future.

I'm a work in progress. We all are, no matter where we find ourselves in the present moment. Think about your own life: What pivotal choices have you made? How do you respond to challenges? Reflect on your journey and consider how each decision has shaped your path. By engaging in this self-reflection, you can begin to understand your own capacity for growth and change.

The journey from confinement to freedom is not just about overcoming physical barriers but also about breaking free from the mental and emotional chains that bind us. Personal liberation is a continuous process of growth, reflection, and transformation. As you read this, I invite you to consider your own path to reclaiming your future. Remember Mandela's words and rise every time you fall. Through resilience and self-discovery, we can all find our way to personal freedom.

Fear less...

Healing is a continuous process, not just a final destination
Source: Photo by Desiree J. Riley

Works Cited

Gålnander, R. (2022, June 12). *'The Anxiety of a Lifetime'—Dealing with Debt in Desistance from Crime*. Retrieved from The British Journal of Criminology, Volume 63, Issue 2, March 2023, Pages 461–476: https://academic.oup.com/bjc/article/63/2/461/6602102.

Guan, N., Guariglia, A., Moore, P., Xu, F., & Al-Janabi, H. (2022, February 22). *Financial stress and depression in adults: A systematic review*. Retrieved from PLOS ONE: https://doi.org/10.1371/journal.pone.0264041.

Reill, A. (2023, December 05). *A Simple Way to Make Better Decisions*. Retrieved from Harvard Business Review: https://hbr.org/2023/12/a-simple-way-to-make-better-decisions.

Chapter 7

It Takes a Village

By Kelsie Becklin, PhD

Introduction to Dr. Kelsie Becklin's Chapter

By Dr. Stanley Andrisse

"You're a single mom, Kelsie. You're older, you have a record, and let's not forget—mental health struggles don't just vanish. Maybe you should rethink this whole grad school thing," someone once told her. Kelsie stared back, her resolve hardening. "Maybe it's not about the odds," she said softly, "but about what happens when I defy them."

For Dr. Kelsie Becklin, the path to higher education was anything but conventional. Her story is a testament to resilience in the face of systemic barriers that too often derail dreams before they begin. A lack of adequate mental health care and substance abuse treatment options has funneled countless individuals into the criminal legal system, effectively criminalizing the struggles that should be met with care and support. Research reveals the devastating impact of untreated mental health issues on recidivism rates and social reintegration. For Kelsie, these challenges were not just statistics—they were her reality.

But Kelsie didn't let her circumstances define her. Despite every obstacle, she pursued her education, an accomplishment

(continued)

(continued)

that flies in the face of studies suggesting that formerly incarcerated individuals, particularly single parents, face insurmountable odds in achieving higher education. "I wouldn't have applied to grad school if I hadn't found Stan online," Kelsie admits. "I wasn't even sure it was legal for someone like me. I Googled people like me—someone with my story who made it anyway—and that's when I found P2P."

Prison to Professionals (P2P) became Kelsie's lifeline, a place where she could shed the social awkwardness of hiding her past and embrace her full self. It wasn't just a community; it was a catalyst. Through P2P, Kelsie found mentors, opportunities, and an entirely new way of seeing her potential. "During grad school, I worked with P2P on projects that were so different from my scientific work. That experience shaped how I mentor others now—it's about being real and showing up for people, no matter where they come from."

Kelsie's journey wasn't without its battles. Balancing the demands of higher education, the stigma of her past, and the challenges of single motherhood often seemed impossible. But Kelsie found strength in rewriting the narrative for herself and for others. As she puts it, "Getting my education wasn't just about me. It was about showing my kids and everyone else that the data doesn't define us."

This chapter explores the deeply intertwined issues of mental health, substance abuse, and the criminal legal system, through the lens of Kelsie's incredible journey. It highlights the systemic barriers faced by justice-impacted individuals and underscores the transformative power of education, mentorship, and community.

Dr. Kelsie Becklin is proof that with the right support, no barrier is insurmountable. Her story is one of triumph, not because the challenges disappeared but because she refused to stop climbing.

My second life started with the words, "This doesn't have to be the end of your life. It can be the beginning of your future. Go make something of yourself." These words were spoken to me by my judge on the day of sentencing. I knew this wasn't normal, but I also took them to heart. He wasn't the first person nor the last who encouraged me to be better, to not let my sentence be the end of my story, but maybe he was the most important one to say it.

So many people hear words of discouragement from a judge. How they will never be better. How they deserve to be locked up and the key thrown away. How a judge may wish they could give a longer sentence but cannot due to guidelines. Or who they are as a person is the problem, and you can't change who you are. So why me? Why was I given words of encouragement that still ring deep in my heart and provided me with motivation when I did not have much else? I still wonder why me? I don't have any answers to this question, but I do know they changed my outlook on the future. I have come to learn that having others believe in you is the first step to change. The second step is believing in yourself. My story is all about the people who fought for me. Those who opened doors and gave me chances. Those, like my judge, who encouraged me to remain strong in the face of adversity. I am writing my story to encourage you to believe in others and to believe in yourself, and forget those who want the worst for you. It is not an easy path, but the view can be beautiful.

Going into court on sentencing day I was nervous, my heart was pounding, I couldn't sit still, and it was so incredibly hot in there. My lawyer assured me we did good and that I would find my sentence tolerable. I was given four months in community confinement and four months on house arrest with a few years on parole. Initially I was told I would have three to five years in federal confinement and at only 21 years old that seemed like forever. I knew I could manage these few months after everything else I went through. Leaving court that day I remember feeling resigned. I wasn't happy, but I was happy it was over. There is this time between being charged with a crime and getting sentenced, I'd call it interstitial time. The time in between. Life pauses. Nothing moves forward. You cannot plan for a future when you don't know you will have one. But now I could, and with the words of encouragement from my judge and all the hard work I had done during my interstitial time, I wasn't sure what it would look like, but I at least felt like I had one. An uncertain one, but a future, nonetheless. I hope my story reminds people to dream big, find solutions, and encourage others; simply don't give up.

My story begins in a loving home, the youngest of five siblings. My parents were both gym teachers. I always felt like they were the cool teachers, the ones you got to have fun with, not the ones who made you sit still all day. I played sports and lived in a neighborhood with a few close friends, one of who still to this day is more like a sister. But like all families we had our share of heartache. In my family this was the loss of my brother Kasey; he was 16, and I was almost 14 when he passed. It wasn't a surprise when he died; he had spent the last few years in and out of the hospital fighting to keep his disabled body alive. My brother kept my family together; he had an incredible gift, the gift of joy, which he gave to the world through his laugh. I would come home from school and call out letting him know I arrived, and he would laugh. Kasey didn't laugh like the rest of us; it was a huge belly laugh that reverberated throughout the entire house. It was the best coming home to his laugh, and I would give anything to hear it again. It's one of those memories that I never thought I would forget, but I can't for the life of me recall his laugh anymore. I can only remember how I felt hearing it, the emotional memory I still have and cherish.

Grief hits everyone differently, and much like I knew that my brother's struggles were bigger than mine I also understood that my parents' grief was too. In the next year my remaining siblings moved out of state to start their lives while I moved on to high school and my parents remained grieving. I was and still am a crazy horse girl, and to help everyone through this time my parents found some friends that were willing to let me ride as much as I wanted if I helped out around the farm. I'm sure they weren't expecting me to come almost every day for the next several years, but I did. Turns out horses really are healers. When I rode, my sadness, loneliness, and confusion all melted away. It was just me and my horse in present time leaving all the pain behind us in our dust trail.

After high school I went to college. My mom talks about the moment we pulled into campus, and I stated that I wasn't ready. I asked them to not leave me there. They did the parent thing and said I was just nervous and that I would soon make friends and be having a great time. I made it a few weeks before the stress became overwhelming and the girl who didn't even drink in high school turned to substances for relief. The summer before college I had my wisdom teeth taken out and was prescribed Percocet, standard practice back then. I remember the warm feeling of bliss when I took the medication; it was so relaxing, and I had never experienced anything like it before. When I went to college and it wasn't going well, I wanted the same feeling. Pain medicines are hard to find though, so I used over-the-counter cough medicine. I would take an entire box and melt into my bed, lost to the world.

Despite playing hockey and living in the dorms, I lost any friendships I could have had due to my abuse of cough meds. I isolated, had emotional outbursts, remained in a constant negative mindset, and pushed anyone away while I simultaneously was screaming for help. Two weeks into my second semester, thinking that ending my life would get me the peace I needed, I took a bunch of pills and wound up in an ambulance being taken to a local hospital that had a mental health ward. When I woke up, I found out I was committed and had to stay for three days, but that turned into months.

During my time there I was given 14 electroconvulsive shock therapy sessions. The doctors told me that they didn't really know how this treatment worked but that they were going to shock my brain into a seizure, and similar to a dead car battery, it seemed to be like a jump start. People would feel like their depressive symptoms would suppress, but one major side effect is you lose all short-term memory. My family would come to visit me, but I couldn't remember. To me I was abandoned. I know they came now, not because I remember but because I have seen my family's commitment to seeing me succeed; there is just no way they didn't come. I often get asked if this treatment worked. Looking back, I'd say it didn't due to the continual struggles I had after leaving the hospital.

Just like on the outside I ended up using horses as my way to keep strong while in the hospital. Every day I was allowed to watch a video a friend had made of the horses. I sometimes wonder what would have happened if I decided to leave and just go ride. But inside those hospital walls, watching the horses on a screen gave me a reason to keep getting better. I would sit and watch the video and feel like I was back riding, the fresh air, the exhilaration, the freedom. I needed to get back to them, to where I was always enough, just as I am.

After my time in the ward the doctors recommended I go to treatment—yes, drug treatment for my abuse of cough medicine. I remember my family doubting the doctors, but I grew up respecting medical professionals, and we didn't push too much. So I went to a 90-day inpatient treatment center, the first of several I attended. I don't remember a single thing about what I learned in treatment except how to do and obtain drugs, which led me to the streets.

I knew I was making bad choices, hanging out in a part of town where drugs were rampant, but I was drinking and smoking weed mostly, nothing that serious at first. My drug buddy always told me to not go out without him, but one day when he was busy, I went out anyway. Someone I had partied with before quickly flagged me down and asked if I was looking to hang out; he knew where everyone was. I quickly said yes and let him in to my car. Immediately I knew something was wrong as he said I needed to go to a place I had never been, and when I hesitated, he pulled up his shirt and I saw it, the silver end of a weapon. I was scared, but decided it was best to not get into an argument, so I brought him to where he wanted to go, hoping when we got there that I could come up with some excuse to leave. When we made it, it was clear that wouldn't happen. I ended up going inside where I was faced with an ultimatum, and I made a choice that I still believe kept me alive. So many people say things about how they would fight till death instead of obliging under these circumstances, but I didn't, and I am proud of the girl I was who kept me safe during the worst events of my life.

Time becomes a confusing thing during life-changing events. The time I spent with these guys seemed to last an eternity, but I later realized it was only two days; it's just that these two days changed my life forever. I had my first hit of crack cocaine. I learned how to work the streets. I had a newfound fear of not listening to men. I began wishing my life would end; I remember praying for it. But then my chance came to get away. I was being moved to a different apartment, and after walking outside, we saw cops at the red light just across the street. The guy transporting me angrily tossed me the keys and said to do exactly what he wanted, mentioning that the cops knew him, so he couldn't drive. This was my chance.

As I pulled out, I didn't use my blinker. I remember worrying that doing so wouldn't be enough to get pulled over, but due to the cop's desire to get the guy with me, they did. I still thought cops were good guys at this point and I felt immediate relief that they were there to help me. Until I met Cop 1. I told him everything that had happened to me over the last two days, and he responded with a laugh and told me, "What did you expect? You're nothing but a crack addict." Did you know that when someone experiences trauma, the way the brain processes it is in part due to the reaction of the "first responder"? The first responder being the person an individual tells a traumatic event to first, it can be family, friends, police, or firefighters ... just the first person you tell. When a first responder reacts appropriately and makes that individual feel safe, then the trauma remains pliable and can integrate into someone's story as they heal. When that doesn't happen, the trauma gets buried in the mind, and that individual will suffer further, in isolation.

Sitting on the curb I met Cop 2, the "good cop." He tried to get me to speak, but I couldn't; the trauma had already set in. I remember he asked me what I was doing there and told me of the young woman who was recently found in the trunk of a car. I reminded him of her he said, and I silently wished I were her. I left this scene not to safety but with a new charge, court date, and need for heavy drugs. I became exactly what Cop 1 said I was.

During the time after this first interaction with the cops and getting into major legal troubles, my life quickly spun out of control. I was fired from many jobs, lost all friends except for my drug buddies, and had many more negative interactions with cops. The most notable to me was a week or so after the first encounter. I was beaten up and left unconscious behind some office buildings; it was a friend of the guy who was arrested that first day. He stole my phone thinking it was his friend's, and his punches were so strong I still have a feeling that something is inside my left ear, like a cotton swab is inside there. When I came to, I jumped up and raced in the direction I saw the guy go right as someone was getting out of their car. I asked them which way he went, and they were confused as they had been parked for their lunch break but didn't see anyone go through the lot. He offered me help, and I went with him into his office to call the cops. I was informed that I could file a report but likely nothing would happen as there weren't any witnesses. I was also told I could go to the hospital for my pounding head, but I was guaranteed to get drug tested and charged with public intoxication if positive. This little threat was enough to keep me on the streets and not go to the one place that could help me. Again, I was failed by my first responders. I was not a victim in their minds, just another street addict.

Despite being heavily on drugs, I still saw my childhood horse, Tommy. I later learned that my parents would call the barn owners and ask if they had seen me. Often that was the only way they knew I was alive. I usually tried to go early in the morning before I would have to talk to anyone else, but the owners would recall seeing my red jacket out in the fields, and my parents would know I was okay. My horse was always my baby. I started riding him when I was 14, and he would come running to the gate when he saw my car. But during my addiction he didn't. I would often spend 30 minutes chasing him just to get his halter on. I don't know, but it seemed like he could tell something was wrong with me, something he and others didn't want to be around. I still think that being a crazy horse girl saved my life during this time. He was my rock, and our near-daily rides got me out of the cities and gave me purpose. I wouldn't have made it without him.

One day my main drug buddy wanted to do something to get a lot of money, and I felt like I had to be there, street rules. I never thought he would do it. I never thought he would actually rob the bank. We had discussed it a few times, but it felt more like a pipedream than real. But when he asked if I "knew a good bank," I thought of one recently built near my hometown that had easy highway access. When I picked him up, we had a 40-minute drive to the bank and we discussed how we would never get away with it, how we should just get sober, and how we could get jobs, and questioned if we were ready to not see our family for years. We never discussed getting away long term, I don't think we ever thought we would get away with it, but we did it anyway. The desire to get drugs was so strong it overrode our sense of logic, and it would be way more money than we usually had. When I pulled up, I parked on the street a good football field away from the door to the bank. He walked out, and I waited in the car. The longer it took him, the more I was convinced he didn't do it, and he just didn't know how to come back to tell me, so I waited. I did think to leave a few times, particularly when a car drove right past me, and I could tell they saw me and recognized that I was acting strange being parked on the street like that. But I stayed and waited. Finally, I saw him come walking down the road, and I was so relieved until he suddenly sprinted to my car. The moment he ran I knew my life as I knew it was over.

I drove away following all traffic rules, but I remember shaking, the panic building in my chest, my inability to breathe, the blurry vision, and the fear. Fear of what was going to happen to me. Do they kill bank robbers on sight? How long will I go to prison? What will my family think? What will I do with my future? What will happen to my horse? So many unanswered thoughts swarmed my head but so did the excitement of knowing we were on our way to get drugs. After securing the drugs, we found a hotel to stay at.

I was so excited to get high I could hardly wait; we had never had this many drugs at one time before. But that feeling of unease and fear, it just never left, and I had the worst trip of my life. I spent nearly the whole time with my eyes locked to the eyepiece in the hotel door, frantically waiting for the cops to show up. Crack wasn't usually something to cause hallucinations, but the combination of drugs and stress does things you don't always expect. I remember how I watched as my drug buddies' skin seemed to melt off and he was left as a skeleton face; it was scary. The remainder of that time is a blur, and when we finally left, we went back to his mom's house where she was waiting, demanding to know why the FBI was looking for us.

His mom drove us to turn ourselves in; she made sure to tell us how loved we were and that we would be okay. It was a tough time waiting on the courts after this, but my lawyer had a plan, and I followed it. I went to treatment, did therapy, got a job, and continued to ride my horse. The very first person to reach out to me when I was home on bail was the owner of the horse farm. She came over to tell me that my horse was waiting for me, and I was welcome at any time, mentioning how I would only heal through the horses. She left me with a huge stack of horse magazines to keep me occupied until I could leave the house. Most people dismiss you in a situation like this but not the horse world; they kept me close and didn't turn their back. I ended up doing a few months in community confinement and then house arrest, which I did at a new partner's apartment in the city, far away from the horses.

When I decided to move home, I remember being scared. I wanted to exit safely with my son, so I planned to leave in the morning before my partner woke up. I didn't have enough gas to get me to my parents' house, but I had some change that I had kept from purchases, and I waited for the bank to open so I could exchange the coins for paper bills. I must have looked like a wreck because the bank teller told me a fable that I wish I could remember but can only remember the meaning, which was "Everyone will disappoint you. It is up to you to determine its impact." These words were spoken in kindness, from a stranger, who only offered hope. It's always best to be kind and offer hope; you never know, it may be a mom struggling to cope with what lays before her, and you may be offering her a chance to overcome the odds yet again.

I drove to my parents after this, really wanting to keep driving but knowing that I should get it over with. I showed up with only my baby and a duffel bag packed with some basic items. When I walked in, my parents were in the kitchen; neither questioned why I was there. The silence was broken with a request about what we should have for lunch later that day, tuna melt or a grilled cheese sandwich. My memory flips a little on what I chose, but I do remember it tasting like the best sandwich I ever had. I am forever grateful to my parents. Not only did they let us live with them, they supported us without complaint and never made me feel like it was my fault; they just continued to show up for us. I hope others are making hard decisions, that they too have the unquestionable support like I did.

Around the time my son was one I had an aha moment. He was playing on the floor, and I was overwhelmed with love for him. He was perfect. I knew he deserved the world, but then it hit me. He has a single mom, recovering from drug addiction, who struggles with mental health, a felony on her record with no skills, no job, and no hope for the future. And his future was completely dependent on mine. Involvement in the criminal legal system spans generations. It doesn't just impact the individual; it impacts everyone around them, most harshly the children. I didn't know this fact at the time, but I could feel it, how he was impacted by choices I made long before he was ever conceived. I had to do something about it; he deserved to have a mom who fought for him in every way possible.

Soon after this revelation I walked into the local community college and met with an advisor after filling out a paper application as I didn't really use technology much. Looking back, I realize how dumb I must have seemed. I went to the meeting with my son in a stroller and immediately asked the advisor what kind of jobs someone with my background can get. He asked a few questions and recommended I don't waste my money on school as I wouldn't likely graduate nor get a job after. I left the meeting not knowing what to do, but then I walked by a computer lab and asked the staff person how to log in and sign up for classes. She mentioned to me that there were services that helped with that, the advisor I just came from, but I said with my son I would prefer to do it here. She helped me get my first two classes scheduled for that summer. I would be starting school again in a few weeks.

I wasn't sure what I could do with a degree yet, but I loved school this time around. Despite knowing that it was unlikely that I could get a nursing degree with my conviction I began with the prenursing program. Mostly because I thought it would be a good job if I could get licensed, and it was just what most nontraditional students did at my school. When my first biology course ended, the professor asked for a meeting. He told me that I wasn't a good nursing student. That most nursing students cared about what they would need to do to help someone with a particular issue, but I was concerned with what caused their problems in the first place. He suggested that I try another biology class, which was not needed for the nursing program. Next semester I did take some classes for the prenursing program, but I also took the next biology course due to his recommendation. The semester after I took only biology courses and quit my prenursing pathway.

I was able to participate in various research projects during my time in community college, but a major change happened the day I walked into my genetics class. I only took this class because in another class we were going to sedate captive wolves to do a basic health exam and collect samples that were to be analyzed in the genetics course. I wanted to see the entirety of the project, so I signed up for both classes. On the first day, my genetics professor was doing introductions, and when she came to me, she said something about how she had heard of me and questioned why I was in her class when historically I was doing ecology research. She teased me about my ability to do genetics. I took the dare and decided I would get the best grade in the class. I am not sure if I got the top grade, but I did fall in love with genetics. I had no clue what we could do with DNA, and I still love finding out.

My genetics professor encouraged me to do a summer internship through a program she ran, a collaboration between the University of Minnesota (UMN) and the community college. During class she always spoke of this one professor at the UMN and how amazing he was. So, I said if I could work for him, I would do the summer internship. She got us a meeting, and after a few minutes I was informed I would be working with a postdoc in the lab for the summer; they had a need, and I was available. At the time I didn't know that this opened door would change the course of my life. It was a door I needed help opening, and I am forever grateful to my genetics professor who believed in me so much she put herself out there to open it and to the UMN professor and his postdoc for taking in a community college student.

During that initial meeting my professor mentioned that I would be attending UMN in the fall and could possibly stay working beyond the summer. This comment really nailed the summer internship. But what she failed to mention was that I was under review by a committee at the university: a committee designed to determine if an applicant who had to check the box, the one you check if you have a felony, was a safety risk to the wider campus community. My application was pending upon their review. I had phone conversations with this committee throughout the summer, and I would get really stressed when they called. But finally, I got word that I was admitted into my chosen college at the UMN just a few weeks before classes were to start. I made it beyond another barrier, another roadblock that most students never had to consider, but I got to celebrate.

My undergrad years were busy. I would get up in the morning and take my son to daycare on my way to school, but usually my parents picked him up. They did this because if I wasn't staying late in the lab, I was going to work as a server at a local restaurant until nearly closing. Some semesters I was so busy I would only see my son a few hours each week. I remember going to the movies a lot because I would take a nap prior to my work shift and still feel like I got to do something "fun" with my son. Even today, when I go to the movies, I almost always fall asleep within a few minutes. As my son got older, I would take him to a trampoline park or indoor playground when I had a big test coming up. We would invite a friend to come with, and they would play all day while I sat at a table with my textbook, trying to cram the information in. I look back on these memories with mixed emotions. I see a mom fighting for her family's future, but I also see missed moments and memories and I wonder if it was all worth it.

Another feeling I had during my undergrad years was the feeling of looking over my shoulder a lot. This feeling never went away in all my years of school. The feeling that someday they will figure out I don't belong there, and my educational journey would be done. But I made it to graduation day already knowing that my next step, graduate school, was just about to start. That feeling of not belonging was what drove me to intensive Google searching prior to applying to grad school to find someone like me: a person with a felony who had a PhD in science. It took quite a bit of Googling back then as most justice-impacted people with PhDs were in social sciences, not biological sciences. But I found him. Dr. Stanley Andrisse, previously incarcerated, had earned his PhD. Furthermore, he was running a research lab at a university alongside being a founding member of a group that supports justice-impacted people pursuing higher education. I was shocked at the time to learn that there were other people like me. Other justice-impacted people fighting the stigma and societal barriers through education. My mind was blown.

After learning of this group, I was still hesitant to get involved in the community, because the risks felt too high. But I could not shake the feeling of knowing there were people like me in higher education; I had never met one. After passing my prelims, I decided I was able to help, so I signed up to be a mentor in the P2P program. Never did I think that this decision would impact me so much. I learned that by mentoring I was also gaining a huge wealth of personal support, information, and the ability to heal. I was able to speak on experiences and be understood for the first time ever, and here my past was not considered shameful, just a part of my story. My story of grit, passion, and being a mom in a world that made it extra difficult for me to pursue higher education. I remain in contact with almost all my past mentees, but now we consider ourselves friends.

During my second half of grad school, I was offered by P2P to lead a program to increase the rates of justice-impacted people pursuing science, technology, engineering, and mathematics (STEM) education and careers. Because of the support from my PhD advisors, I was able to take this project on, and it forever shaped my career. I got the best education on leading a team of people and making high-end decisions on a project firsthand. It gave me the confidence I needed in my science career to be a leader and the passion to continuing mentoring people. Even after I had to step down, I remained in close contact with most of my group members, and some have even become my best friends and the people I lean on during hard times. I still feel most comfortable being myself with other justice-impacted people because we form a community that has yet to let me down.

I continue to mentor P2P scholars working to better their lives through higher education, and I enjoy participating in programs offered through the justice-impacted community. I haven't landed the dream job I earned my PhD for yet, but I find that working in the university system gives me a lot to be grateful for. I get to do some of the most cutting-edge research on childhood cancer, HIV/AIDS, and other rare diseases with a focus on improving the safety and efficacy of future therapies. I am involved in mentoring the next generation of scientists. I get to communicate with a wide variety of audiences on the importance of my field. And I am thinking about teaching at a community college or starting an equine therapy center for trafficked and abused people. It is in these spaces where I think I can have the most impact on a person like me. Maybe I can be the one who opens doors to a new career or helps someone heal through the power of horses. Honestly, I am unsure of where I will end up, I have a lot of ideas I want to pursue, but I know that the P2P community, my justice-impacted friends, and my family will support whatever I chose, and they will be at the heart of what I do. My story is nothing if it doesn't inspire and help someone be different. I don't believe in second chances, but I do believe that we should meet someone where they are. So, if they come in different that day, I should meet them there, in the new world that each of us wakes up too every day, carrying the experiences that changed us from the day before. So, it is not second chances, but it is really hundreds, thousands, millions of chances for those that are making the hard choices to be better today than yesterday. Thank you to my parents who gave me all the chances I needed, and thank you to my son who never thought I needed a second one.

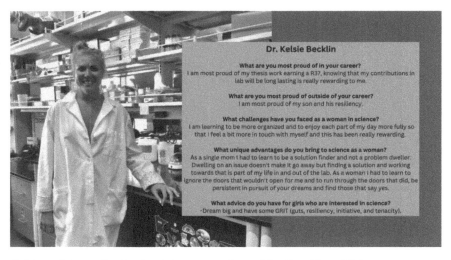

Kelsie, a biomedical scientist, was pardoned by President Biden
Source: Photo by Dr. Kelsie L. Becklin

Chapter 8

A House Made of Ashes

By Elhadji Ndiaye

Introduction to Elhadji Ndiaye's Chapter

By Dr. Stanley Andrisse

"Growing up, it felt like poverty was a shadow, always present, always looming," Elhadji Ndiaye reflects. "But shadows only exist when there's light—and I decided to chase that light, no matter how far away it seemed."

For Elhadji, poverty wasn't just a backdrop to his life; it was a driving force, shaping choices and circumstances that ultimately led to his involvement with the criminal legal system. Economic hardship has long been recognized as a key driver of incarceration, disproportionately impacting marginalized communities. Studies consistently show that individuals from low-income backgrounds are at a higher risk of incarceration, often due to survival-based offenses and systemic inequities. But Elhadji's story doesn't end with statistics—it's one of defiance, resilience, and transformation.

Enrolled at Howard University via the Prison to Professionals (P2P) NIH-funded Bridges to Baccalaureate program, and set to graduate in 2028, Elhadji's journey is a testament to perseverance against overwhelming odds. "The path hasn't been easy," he

(continued)

(continued)

admits, "but with the right guidance, I've learned that what seemed like barriers were really just opportunities to grow stronger."

That guidance came, in part, from P2P. "Stan and P2P have been instrumental," Elhadji shares. "They didn't just provide assistance; they helped me reimagine what was possible. From professional development to personal growth, the support I've received has been life-changing."

Through P2P, Elhadji found not only resources but a community that believed in his potential. The organization's holistic approach to mentorship and advocacy emphasizes addressing systemic inequities like poverty, which disproportionately funnel individuals into the criminal justice system. P2P's work is grounded in the belief that education and opportunity are the most powerful tools for breaking cycles of incarceration.

This chapter delves into the intersection of poverty and incarceration, using Elhadji's experiences to illustrate how economic hardship often dictates life trajectories. But more importantly, it showcases how access to education and mentorship can rewrite those trajectories entirely.

"Howard University isn't just a milestone," Elhadji says. "It's a promise—to myself, my family, and everyone who believed in me—that I'll keep chasing the light."

Elhadji's story reminds us that no shadow is permanent and that with the right support, even the most daunting barriers can become stepping stones toward a brighter future.

Systemic poverty not only shaped my environment but also set the stage for the cycles of incarceration that followed. From a young age, survival was my primary focus, and the instability of my upbringing often placed me in situations where the criminal justice system became an inevitable force in my life. Whether through the lack of resources, the exposure to violence, or the absence of support structures, poverty created the conditions that made incarceration not just a possibility but a near certainty.

Growing up in shelters, group homes, and unstable housing wasn't just a backdrop to my story—it was the foundation of a cycle that seemed impossible to escape. Poverty wasn't just about lacking money; it shaped every decision, every opportunity, and every outcome. When survival is the priority, long-term goals fade into the background. The streets become both a refuge and a battlefield, where mentorship often comes from those navigating the same struggles, reinforcing patterns that lead to incarceration rather than breaking them. Like so many others, I wasn't given a roadmap to success—only a series of obstacles disguised as reform. The juvenile detention centers, the so-called rehabilitation programs, and the revolving doors of shelters didn't offer solutions; they only deepened my entrapment in the system. Incarceration wasn't a sudden fall—it was a slow, inevitable pull, shaped by the instability of my early years and the absence of real opportunities to escape the fire I was born into.

A House Made of Ashes

"No pain, no gain" is a saying that implies the gain is worth the pain. But that applies only if you want something badly enough to endure the discomfort. Most people don't. They stand like dreamers staring at distant stars, at least I have for a long time, and paralyzed by how far away their goals seem. But passion—real, burning passion—changes everything. It pushes us to reach for the impossible. There is no fulfillment without passion, and without it, we'll never withstand the obstacles between us and our desires. We must want it badly enough to survive the process of attaining it. That's what Deion, an incarcerated person at United States Prison (USP) Atlanta, wrote in his essay called "A House Made of Ashes." You see, Deion, like me, had been in and out of the mass industrial incarceration complex his whole life. Similar to Deion, I was in shelter homes, group homes, juvenile detention centers, and hospitalized on numerous occasions. Each place was in the namesake of reforming him, but just like me, it was to no avail. On my way to stand before a jury trial for murder, the *United States of America vs. Elhadji B. Ndiaye*, held in the District of Columbia, I was passing through Atlanta USP. It is there that Deion explained his philosophy to me about how we all are in that burning house Dr. Martin Luther King was talking about before he was assassinated.

The fire roared.

The air was thick with smoke.

Lights flashed.

I heard a paralyzing scream, but I kept going.

"Don't stop throwing water!" Mom's voice rang out, steady through the chaos. My heartbeat pounds through the fire; the heat tickles my pores. My mother's fear is carved into her face. Shots rang out during the day, more frequently by night. There is no place to play, success is going away they say, but this is my home. A place of danger and survival. Firefighters crashed through my bedroom windows. Fire—madness. You have to see it to understand it. I saw it, and I vanished, like smoke. A part of me switched into sport mode, surviving, saving the day. I'm the hero now, or at least I try to be. I landed on Pluto just to have a conversation with my future. I'm anxious, but I know tomorrow is another day. I left my spare key under the mat never to return to my house made of ashes.

My name is Elhadji Babacar Ndiaye. Very hard to pronounce and harder to understand. My name is in the Quran and the Bible. Elhadji means God knows me. The name was selected by my biological father Oumar. At the time, 1999, to be precise, the doctors and nurses couldn't pronounce it. Even my mother had trouble with the sound.

At School Without Walls, a prestigious area in Capitol Hill, there were more than 10 Elhadji's, all spelled completely differently. My name started getting popular just after five years or so.

One of my best friends, named Raquan Williamson but better known as G-Feet, was gunned down three years ago—I know he's really dead because he hasn't come to check on me. Part of me is still waiting on him. He was one of the strongest War Time Generals in DC. People from all over the city would head to his counsel and seek his aid. No amount of revenge could recover the loss obtained by his passing. He was murdered execution style. His vehicle was boxed in, he received an onslaught of bullets. There were many speculations and opinions after his passing. Many say it was his fault: he should have been paying attention, he should have been using his mirrors, but in all actuality G-Feet was a problem that needed to be dealt with. I believe death is strange: so many people were shaken up by his death because no one expected someone so strong and powerful to be killed like that. One of my favorite quotes on death is "Everybody knows they're going to die, but nobody believes it." Raquan is leaving behind a brother and three loving sisters, his parents, and a lot of friends who all genuinely love and care for him.

G-Feet was a transformational leader and an individual who focused on helping every member of the group. The Boss, Head Honcho, Shot Caller, Sayso ... many people have filled those shoes, and most if not all are incarcerated. Unfortunately, too many of these leaders are "finished seeing outside" or no longer here with us. It appears to me that I do not believe I am a street veteran by far. The veterans who I have been acquainted with are much more humbled and accomplished in life. The pains, struggles, degradation, and time produced a type of patience these leaders had and can only be explained by the time. I'll say that from my observation the thickness of war and peace dances in the air, and when people die or are killed, that could make those steps toward peace and forgiveness

A House Made of Ashes

turn into weights that become heavier and heavier from each passing. All kin on both sides are affected. G-Feet leaves behind many soldiers and comrades all whom needed his guidance and inspiration. He was only 24 years old. His potential was limitless, and he had already maintained a strong control and influence on both parts of the biggest wars going on in the District.

I take full responsibility for the passing of my friend. I sat by and watched him make terrible decisions. I encouraged, supported, funded, and protected his entire empire of violence. Raquan's journey was marked by challenges and turmoil; unfortunately, he is not here to explain. When we sit face-to-face with the Ultimate Father, we will answer for what is done on Earth. Will we take accountability or shy away? My fate was already declared long ago. The only thing I can do now is focus on my purpose and plan. When you lose someone like that, there is a deep kind of evil that can awaken if not careful. I say this now, to his attackers, it is a struggle, but I make an effort every second that goes by to forgive you. As I continue to forgive those involved in this hideous crime, I win for myself and for my best friend Raquan.

Five years fighting a murder charge in DC. Fighting a global pandemic and fighting for my life. How did I get here, sitting in this cell, staring at these four walls? My soul says to break, but my heart says to keep going. No weapons, no friends, no money, just a pen lying silently on the floor. So, I began to write. Write, read, read, write, read, write, write, and read.

I was born in a military hospital in Bethesda, Maryland: Bethesda Medical Center. The president of the United States was admitted to this hospital. My grandfather Samuel was in the military as a sergeant. He worked at the original Walter Reed Medical Center located on Georgia Ave. N.W. Washington, DC. When my mom Priscilla was 10 years old, the cafeteria was her favorite place to visit in Walter Reed. My mother attempted to have an abortion twice, but I was too far along for the procedure. I was destined to be born. Therefore, starting out 1-0 isn't bad for the new kid. I don't think she was wrong in her decision. She knew it would be tough raising a Black man in this world. Under our conditions in 1999 not much has changed. We permanently moved into the District of Columbia soon after I was born, bouncing from "My Sister's Place" shelter. My mother and I remained in the shelter after I was born and shortly moved to transitional housing in Livingston Road Southeast border line of Oxon Hill, Maryland. Home, life, humanity, or peace—whichever was cheaper. She and I dealt with a lot because she lived a life as a single Black female. I involuntarily took the role of man of the house. My early years were a brawl. My mother did her very best working one full-time job, a few part-time jobs, and putting herself in school. I was a little Black boy whose father never picked him up from school. I was engulfed in school. When I got home, it was another school ... home school. I had to read, read the dictionary, learn history, Pan Africanism, math, and anything my mother presented to me. Her family had abandoned her, and those relationships are still a work in progress. (Don't act like y'all don't have drama too.) However, with all the hardship, my mother, Priscilla, and her partner, whom I considered my stepdad, stressed the importance of education: seek and find it no matter the cost.

Fellas, we got to do more for our Black women. Women in general are battered with the plight of this life on top of being a woman. The setbacks they experience on top of stress can cause them to put those frustrations on children, which can be a determining factor to shattered childhoods.

I stayed in trouble, and my mama stayed whooping my ass. This made me very shy and unsure of myself. I began feeling confident only when I caused harm to others or even myself. One of my most embarrassing moments was early 2000s. It was the night *High School Musical 2* premiered on Disney Channel. I was at the ARCH/Ms.

Hawkins's house, a recreation center in Southeast DC less than a block from my house at the time. This house was always buzzing—fights, food, games, crimes, gifts, activities, take-home bags, and even the occasional extreme flirtation. Above all else, it did its job, which was to provide a safe place for youth to go after school in the District of Columbia. Specifically on this day, the girl I had the biggest crush on asked me to kiss her. My heart stopped. I couldn't process what she said. So I asked the dumbest question, "Why?" I dislike myself for it. She replied, "Because I know you want to." What did I do? I told her I could not because I was sick. I'm still haunted by that moment. It wasn't about the kiss—it was about fear. Fear is false, evidence appearing real. Fear paralyzes you and stops you from taking action. I think back to what the late Ermias Joseph Asghedom aka Nipsey Hussle said once when asked by an interviewer, "What would you do differently if you could do it over?" "If I could do it over, I'd be more fearless," he replied.

I've always been a strategic planner. I was lonely as a child, so I created an imaginary friend to tell me everything I wanted to hear. It turns out when I got older and learned more about how the brain works and its different components and its many intricacies, I was considered to be "neurodivergent." I was not neurotypical. More specifically, later in life, I was diagnosed with personality disorder. This, of course, being unbeknownst to little me, I created an imaginary friend. I couldn't control what my imaginary friend Jonathan thought. His opinion of things and his actions I could not control. Jonathan was supposed to be Jona, a girl I had a crush on but didn't know how to talk to. Jona was supposed to tell me everything I wanted to hear. Instead, I ended up with a guy named Jonathan. He had an attitude problem and would tell me exactly what I didn't want to hear, but most of the time he was always on point.

Jonathan said something that stuck with me one night in a whisper. I heard him say, "If you pay attention to your mistakes, you can see the next one coming before it happens." "That's how you can see into the future." At the time I struggled to understand exactly what he meant. In essence he was the one who said put your hands on the steering wheel of your life. My question to him was, "Where is the steering wheel?" It's now that I realized that the steering wheel of life was choices.

Fast-forward to high school. My future felt like prison to me. I personally turned down an offer to join an Advanced English class in my senior year, 2017. I didn't have time for that. I had a drug business to run. I gave half my energy to everything, never focusing on what I truly wanted. My thoughts on school at that time were that educational professionals and emeritus professors can teach you a lot, but they can't teach you how to take life seriously. Countless things haunt me. I developed a habit of always trying to make others proud (my mom, my stepdad, my homies in the streets) but never focusing on myself.

Escaping the Ashes

On February 22, 2022, I was released from the District of Columbia Correctional Facility after three years. I was placed on High-Intensity Electronic Monitoring with a 24-hour home confinement order. That is when I met my P2P family. I had heard about P2P through a flyer in the DC Jail, and I had become familiar with the book *From Prison Cells to PhD: It is Never Too Late to Do Good*. I clearly remember being introduced to Dr. Stanley's story of daily persistence and triumph. The organization's philosophies gave me hope. I fell in love with Dr. Stanley's story. His story was my story, and I was determined to learn how to be powerful, impactful, and an influential leader in any environment. My thinking became limitless; my mind was growing. Additionally, creativity, managing my emotions, managing artists, and managing my business were effortless. While incarcerated, I made a plan. I was going to start a marketing business and pursue a career in the music industry. Of course, plans can change or become flexible. I knew my plan, and I pursued my plan vehemently. I learned I like planning years in advance and executing those plans excites me.

I wanted to observe, evaluate, and execute my plans. The top of the list was that I needed to push positively in everything that I do moving forward. With great success comes risk. Henceforth, in August 2022, I took a risk and went to Atlanta, Georgia, breaching the 24-hour electronic monitoring, which required me to stay in DC. Interestingly, I breached the order of confinement to follow my dreams. Through one of my connections, I had an opportunity for a prestigious internship with Tyler Perry. I wanted to find out what Tyler Perry could offer me and what I could offer Mr. Perry's studios. At the time, I was scheduled to stand trial for murder in 2024. Sometimes, the individuals locked up are handled quicker than the defendants in the public. In an act of rebellion, I broke free in the middle of the night, and I disappeared and went to Atlanta. All parties were disappointed in me. Technically, still fighting my case, why would I risk it? I did it because I knew I had to break free or remain a prisoner forever.

Now, I'm focused on the future. I'm studying at Howard University, the nation's leading historical Black college, pursuing a bachelor's degree in the fields of science and law. My plans are to continue my secondary education in the PhD program here too. In addition, I am owner/CEO of EBN Firm, a new startup international acquisition investment conglomerate company in the investment world. While it may be challenging to show up as my authentic self, I believe in prayer and that no human was created for nothing, and we should understand each and every one of us has a purpose to fulfill.

"On February 2, following a multi-week long trial, a homicide defendant was partially acquitted of all charges before

DC Superior Court Judge Anthony Epstein. Elhadji Ndiaye, 24, was acquitted of first-degree murder while armed, possession of a firearm during a crime of violence, tampering with physical evidence, and destruction of property, in connection to the death of 21-year-old Travis Ruth on the 2700 block of Jasper Street, NE on January 18, 2019. However, the jury was hung on the robbery while armed charge and the obstruction of justice. Throughout the trial, Ndiaye's defense attorney, Nikki Lotze, said that Ndiaye was not on the scene when the incident occurred and that two other eyewitnesses tried to cover the murder and pin it on the defendant. Lotze gave three reasons on why the jury should doubt the prosecution's case. She claimed that there was a lack of forensic evidence, a lack of evidence that proves Ndiaye was in the alley at the time of the shooting, and that the Metropolitan Police Department (MPD) failed to investigate this case thoroughly. Prosecutors tried to prove Ndiaye's guilt by presenting witnesses who delivered emotional testimonies. The prosecution's rebuttal to defense' claim that two eyewitnesses were the ones who pinned Ruth's murder on Nidaye was that they were very close friends of the victim. The two eyewitnesses spent a lot of time with Ruth and his family and have had dinner with the Ruth family on several occasions, the prosecution claimed. During the prosecution's closing statement, they referenced the second day of trial, when the victim's mother greeted one of the eyewitnesses outside of the courtroom with a hug. The prosecution argued, how could the mom of a son who was brutally murdered hug their killer? After the intense trial and days of deliberations, a jury of 12 found Ndiaye not guilty of murdering Ruth, and were unable to conclude if he was involved in the robbery and obstruction of justice."[1]

Elhadji Ndiaye

Elhadji's illustrated memory of things he experienced at five years old
Source: Photo by Elhadji Ndiaye

Part III
Education and Mentorship

Chapter 9

Fallen

By Lisa and Rachel Guirsch-Webb

Introduction to Lisa & Rachel Guirsch-Webb's Chapter
By Dr. Stanley Andrisse

It was a quiet evening when I first spoke with Rachel and Lisa. Their words crackled over the phone line, heavy with the weight of lives lived under relentless scrutiny. Rachel's voice was measured, a delicate balance of vulnerability and resolve. "Starting college," she said, her tone soft but firm, "that was my rebellion."

Lisa, on the other hand, spoke with an edge, her words like sparks catching fire. "I made it out alive," she said, almost daring me to flinch. "That's my accomplishment—staying alive when everything around me was designed to kill me, if not physically, then spiritually."

Their stories didn't just resonate—they reverberated, striking chords of shared struggle and the determination to transform. They are emblematic of a system that punishes the most vulnerable for their vulnerability. Poverty, mental illness, substance abuse—these aren't mere footnotes in their stories; they are the ink that penned the opening chapters.

As Lisa once confided, "Poverty doesn't just limit your options—it steals your future before you even know you have

(continued)

(continued)

one." Rachel added, "And when you try to self-medicate the pain, they call it a crime. When you get caught, they call it justice."

Lisa and Rachel's narratives are woven into the fabric of a system that thrives on over-policing communities, criminalizing mental illness, and imposing draconian sentencing policies. It's a system Michelle Alexander describes as "The New Jim Crow," where the carceral state replaces the chains of old.

But this isn't just about the system; it's about how they refused to be defined by it.

Rachel's decision to start college while incarcerated was not just an act of defiance—it was a declaration of hope. "Education became my light," she told me. "It was the one thing they couldn't take away." For Lisa, survival meant more than enduring; it meant holding onto the parts of herself that the system tried to erase. She spoke often of her marriage, hidden because of a policy that sought to make her love invisible. "It was a prison within a prison," Lisa admitted.

Through their journeys, they found Prison to Professionals (P2P)—not as a solution, but as a space where solutions could be imagined. "Stan," Rachel said once, "you led the way. You showed me that people like us can be more than what we've been told we are." Lisa echoed the sentiment. "You gave us hope when it felt like there wasn't any left."

Their chapter in this book isn't just about their struggles; it's about the resilience born from them. It's about how Rachel and Lisa turned their incarceration into a foundation for empowerment, using their pain to fuel their purpose.

In their words and their journey, you'll find echoes of countless others who have fallen but dared to rise. And you'll see what happens when two women refuse to let a system designed to break them steal their futures—or their voices.

> As Ta-Nehisi Coates reminds us in *Between the World and Me*, "You must struggle to remember this past in all its nuance, error, and humanity ... because it is the key to the future." Rachel and Lisa's story is both a reckoning with that past and a bold step toward the future.

Fallen Part 1: Rising from the Ashes: Lisa's Journey of Redemption

By Lisa Guirsch-Webb

Suicide Mission

In the summer of 2015, I found myself cornered in every sense of the word. At 33, I was a fugitive, wanted in Oregon, and had spent 18 months hiding in a small coastal town, running from the inevitable. My life had spiraled into chaos, and I was facing 10 years behind bars if caught. That October, with law enforcement closing in on me, I decided it was time to end the suffering in what I saw as the only way left—a suicide mission. When the police surrounded the house, I had every intention of making them pull the trigger.

    I should step back and provide a bit of context. On Mother's Day 2013, I found myself in Klamath County Jail, with no way out. Bail was too high, and circumstances were too volatile. I was tired of getting my ass beat every single day of my life. I had been in a 10-year relationship with a narcissistic alcoholic where every time I left him, he would hunt me with a chainsaw and duct tape, terrorizing everyone I had ever known. With a bounty on my head, I ran from him until I caught charges and spent six months in jail. In December, I was offered a 120-month sentence, which I fought hard to get suspended, with the agreement that I would move to Washington state, and Klamath County would never see my face again. The DA told me to take the deal, or she would charge me with every crime that came across her desk that spring. I took it, and she retired. I moved, and Linda Tolliver from Pacific County Parole and Probation violated my suspended sentence, so I decided to go on the run in this little coastal town until I was surrounded at the end of July 2015.

Back to the summer of 2015, as I stood in a standoff, phone in hand, ready to make my final move, I called my mother. Her voice, fraught with fear and love, was the only connection I had to humanity. In the background, I heard my younger brother, a decorated war veteran who didn't even live in that town, calling out my name. He happened to have been in that town because he had come to visit my mom earlier that day. He lived two hours away, and I thought he had already left town. The police had me surrounded on the other side of town. I didn't know he was outside, pleading with the officers not to kill me. Hearing him shattered the fog of despair. I couldn't let the police shoot me in front of him. Somehow, I found the strength to surrender. As they cuffed me, the officers allowed me one final moment with him. I hugged him, sobbing uncontrollably, apologizing for the pain I'd caused. He didn't say a word then, nor did he answer any of my letters during the years I spent locked up. But that moment planted a seed of change deep within me.

After my arrest, I was taken to the hospital for medical clearance. As desperate as I was to escape my fate, I ran from the hospital, driven by instinct rather than logic. Two weeks later, they caught me. That time, there was no escape. The system swallowed me whole, sentencing me to 57 months in Washington State prison and an additional 63 months in Oregon—a combined 10 years.

Devastation and a Ray of Hope

Two months into my time at Washington Corrections Center for Women (WCCW), my world was rocked again. I called my mother, and to my dismay, I was informed that she had been diagnosed with stage 3 cervical cancer. She couldn't choke the words out, or say them out loud to me that she had stage 3 cancer, so she handed the phone to my stepdad, and he told me. I begged him not to let her die while I was there. It was a very unfair position to put him in. These words crushed me in a way prison never could. I couldn't breathe; every moment felt like my soul was being ripped apart. That New Year's Eve, as panic consumed me, a guard named Sgt. Chanel went out of her way to help. On her break, she walked me to the medical unit, where I met a phlebotomist who used to work in my mom's oncologist's office. That small act of kindness saved my sanity.

Over the next six months, I clung to faith as my lifeline. I spent almost every waking moment in the prison chapel. I attended every service, regardless of denomination or religion, and enrolled in seminary school through a college in Texas. My desperation fueled an unshakable determination—I had more than 30,000 people praying for my mother, and I was determined to make God hear her name. Those prayers must have worked because, despite multiple surgeries and relapses, my mother has been cancer-free for five years now.

A Childhood of Chaos

My journey to that coastal town and that 2015 standoff started long before adulthood. Born into dysfunction, I grew up navigating a turbulent family life. My father was an abusive alcoholic who drank his talent away. He was the lead singer and lead guitarist in a band, and a master contractor. My mother was too young and inexperienced to provide stability. She left me with my grandparents for a few years, but when she returned, she introduced Marty, the man who would adopt me and try to instill some structure in my life. Despite his best efforts, my rebellious nature wore him down. Marty wanted me, loved me, and adopted me, and I put him through living hell. I never had any discipline in my life, and I was a very ungrateful, unruly, disrespectful child, and I cannot blame him for throwing his hands up after years of putting up with my BS because he lasted a lot longer than I would have. I have recently rekindled a relationship with him, which has filled the void I have carried now for decades without him. But, by 14, I was running the streets, using meth, and earning a juvenile record.

At 18, I tried to enlist in the military, passing the ASFAB with flying colors. But my juvenile felony barred me from service. Rejected, I turned back to the streets, starting a cycle of arrests, probation violations, and brief stints in jail. Law enforcement knew me so well they often didn't bother to handcuff me until we got to the station. Jail became my second home, but I was always on the run, calling the station every few weeks to check if I had a warrant. My life was a revolving door of poor choices and fleeting moments of hope dashed by systemic barriers.

A Tale of Two Prisons

Prison in Washington was a challenge, but it gave me opportunities to grow. I became a GED math teacher and lived in a dormitory that allowed me some semblance of normalcy. But when I was transferred to Oregon, everything changed. Prison in Oregon felt like "dead time"—unproductive and stagnant. Education was limited to correspondence courses that cost $600 each, an amount few inmates could afford. It was here that I first saw Rachel. Just a glimpse of her in the hallway was enough to make me pause. I almost turned around to follow her, but I didn't. Not yet.

When I landed in minimum custody, I started to find a rhythm again. I was teaching, staying out of trouble, and rebuilding myself. But in 2019, a disciplinary infraction sent me back to medium custody. That's when our paths finally crossed. I commandeered a table in the H unit, where we lived, unknowingly sitting at Rachel's table. Our connection was immediate, but Rachel, grappling with her own identity, kept her distance. I chased her around the kitchen, trying to talk to her, but she always evaded me. After a month, I was sent back to minimum. If Rachel had asked me to stay, I would have gone back to solitary confinement just to be near her.

Love in the Time of COVID

When COVID-19 shut down the prison system in 2020, everything changed again. Visitation ceased, religious services stopped, and we were confined to our bunks for most of the day. Then, the wildfires hit Oregon, forcing an evacuation to a men's minimum-security facility in Madras. By sheer chance—or maybe fate—I ran into Rachel there. I asked her when she was transferring back to minimum, and two months later, she arrived. This time, we were placed in bunks next to each other. Our bond deepened, and we secretly got married, defying the prison's strict policy against inmate relationships. The policy forbidding romantic relationships between incarcerated people can be found in O.A.R 291-0005. No one knew, not the DOC, not the other inmates. It was our secret, our sanctuary.

We signed up for every college course we could, determined to build a future together. When COVID-19 and staff shortages threatened to separate us again, I pulled every string I could to keep us close. They put me and about 100 others on the move list to go back to medium to be housed, and Rachel wasn't on the move list. I flipped a script and went into the lieutenant's office, and basically gave him an ultimatum. "Either put Rachel on the move list with me, or take me off the list. Please do not make me act up, because I will lock this prison down." I figured I would go to the hole with that threat, but I didn't. He put Rachel on the list. A sympathetic captain even placed us in the same cell for months before returning us to minimum custody, where we continued our journey side-by-side.

Freedom and the Fight for a Future

When Rachel was released two weeks before me, my heart ached with both pride and longing. Upon my release, I paroled to Red Lodge Transition Services, a culturally specific program for Native Americans. Rachel stayed with her aunt and uncle until we could reunite. Those early months were filled with challenges, but we were determined to build a life together.

We dove into education and advocacy, taking AmeriCorps positions to build Project Rebound on the Portland State University campus. Already admitted to PSU before my release, I threw myself into academia. But the system wasn't designed to support people like us. We were tokenized—used as the face of diversity for grants and funding but given little meaningful guidance. The liberal studies pathway we were funneled into wasted time and resources, leaving us feeling betrayed. That's when we resolved to change the system, making Project Rebound of Oregon a beacon of hope and support for justice-impacted individuals.

Finding a Mission with P2P

In October 2022, while attending the National Conference on Higher Education in Prison (NCHEP), I first connected with Dr. Stanley Andrisse through the Whova app. Reading his book, *From Prison Cells to PhD*, ignited a fire in me. Here was someone who had walked a path similar to mine and achieved a level of success I had only dreamed of. When I finally met him and the P2P team in person, it felt like coming home.

I was star-struck and in awe by his background, his story, and by him. I wanted what he had, which was the ability to be successful in his own life, while carving out pathways for others to do the same. At that moment, I knew I could reach the stars too, even though I had not even seen them since around the time I was adopted. I was on a mission to be a catalyst of change, and I knew that with him I could be.

Rachel and I joined the P2P Scholar Program, immersing ourselves in its resources and community. We graduated as scholars, armed with the tools to turn our struggles into a mission. Meeting Dr. Andrisse face-to-face in Washington, DC, was a pivotal moment. He exemplified what it meant to rise above adversity, and his unwavering dedication to helping others inspired us to do the same.

Defying the Odds

Today, Rachel and I are still together, defying the odds stacked against prison relationships. We complement each other in ways I never thought possible, finishing each other's sentences and building a life rooted in love and resilience. We're saving to buy our first home, a testament to the stability we've created together.

Our journey has been far from easy, but it's shaped us into advocates, leaders, and role models. From serving on committees and boards to mentoring others through Project Rebound and P2P, we're driven by a shared mission to dismantle the barriers that keep justice-impacted individuals from reaching their full potential. Every step we take is a tribute to the strength we found in each other and the hope that organizations like P2P provide.

Rachel often says, "If we can survive prison, we can survive anything." And she's right. Together, we're not just surviving—we're thriving.

Fallen Part 2: Love in a Hopeless Place

By Rachel Guirsch-Webb

Introduction

When I fell, I didn't just stumble—I plummeted. It was the kind of fall that shatters everything: your pride, your hope, your sense of who you are. It started with small cracks in my life—unnoticed by most, ignored by me—and ended in a full-blown collapse. Arrests. Courtrooms. Chains around my wrists and ankles. The sound of a gavel crashing down.

I used to think I was strong, invincible even. But there I was, sitting in a county jail, stripped of everything. They tell you that incarceration is about justice, about rehabilitation. What they don't tell you is how it's designed to destroy you from the inside out.

Lisa had her own story of falling. I didn't know her back then, but her pain mirrored mine. She'd hit rock bottom too, spiraling into a system that labels you by your worst moment and forgets the rest.

We met at Coffee Creek Correctional Facility, a place where hope is scarce and humanity even scarcer. But something incredible happened there. In the place where we were supposed to lose ourselves entirely, we found each other—and, somehow, found a way to rise.

Inside Coffee Creek

Walking into Coffee Creek was like stepping into a different world—a cold, gray world designed to remind you at every turn that you were no longer a person. You were an inmate, a number. Nothing more.

Lisa always said it felt like being buried alive, and she wasn't wrong. Every rule, every guard's glare, every tiny indignity was a shovel of dirt thrown on top of us. "They don't just take your freedom," she once told me. "They take everything that makes you feel human."

For me, it was the isolation that broke me. You're surrounded by people, but you've never felt more alone. The walls keep you in, but they also keep love, hope, and any sense of normalcy out.

The Wildfire Evacuation

The wildfires came without warning. I was working in the infirmary when I first caught wind of it—quite literally. The air was thick with smoke, seeping into every corner of the facility. I overheard whispers about an evacuation, but the staff told me to keep quiet.

"Don't say anything," they said. "It'll just cause chaos."

Chaos came anyway. Within hours, we were lined up, handcuffed, and shoved onto buses. I was on a high-security bus, and Lisa was on a minimum-security bus. On the high-security bus, the guards were so terrified of us that they stood the entire ride, backs to the windshield, watching us like we might explode at any moment.

I rode to Deer Ridge Correctional Institution (DRCI) with armed guards, shackled on a high-security transport. Lisa was transported on a school bus with school bus drivers that were more scared of incarcerated individuals than they were of the wildfires. There were no handcuffs or shackles ... for Lisa. She was simply zip-tied at the wrists to her bunkmate. She could just slip them off. They all could. And did. Of course no one tried to run. This was not an escape attempt.

We met up again at the facility we were relocated to. We ate a meal together and talked for hours. The smoke outside was suffocating, but sitting next to her, something shifted. Lisa and I sat together, not saying much at first, just breathing each other's air. When she finally spoke, it wasn't about the fire or the guards or even the evacuation. It was about life—about surviving this place, about what might come next.

That conversation was the first time I felt like maybe, just maybe, I wasn't completely alone.

The Pandemic and Isolation

When COVID-19 hit, I thought we'd already seen the worst Coffee Creek had to offer. I was wrong.

The lockdowns made a bad situation unbearable. No visitors. No programs. No outside contact. The isolation was suffocating. For months, we lived in a bubble of fear and silence.

I saw the worst of it in the infirmary. People were getting sick, and we didn't have the resources to help them. Ventilators became a lifeline, but even then, there wasn't enough. I remember watching someone struggle for air and thinking, This can't be it. This can't be how we live—how we die.

Lisa kept me grounded during those months. She'd write me notes, little reminders that we were still in this together. "One day at a time," she'd say. It was a mantra that kept us both alive.

Love in a Hopeless Place

Lisa and I didn't fall in love the way people imagine. It wasn't some grand, romantic moment. It was quiet, cautious—a bond forged in survival.

When they finally moved me next to Lisa in dorm 400, we were like two giddy school girls. We stayed up all night, all day, and didn't sleep much for like 21 days or something. Too excited to finally be around each other. No one else existed. I'm sure our side bunkies and most of the unit hated us for talking and laughing all night.

At first, we were just friends, helping each other navigate the unspoken rules of prison life. But over time, that friendship deepened. Lisa became my anchor, my safe place.

When we decided to get married, it wasn't about defying the system or making a statement. It was about us—about holding onto something real in a place that felt so unreal.

Education: A Light in the Darkness

If love kept us grounded, education gave us wings.

I still remember the day Lisa convinced me to sign up for the college program. I'd written it off as a waste of time, something the system dangled in front of us to look good on paper.

"You're smarter than you think," she told me. "And you've got nothing to lose."

She was right. The first time I turned in a paper and got feedback, something in me lit up. For the first time in years, I felt like I had a future—a life beyond these walls.

We studied together, staying up late to help each other with assignments. Those nights were our escape, our way of reclaiming the parts of ourselves the system had tried to erase.

Reentry: One Step at a Time

When I walked out of Coffee Creek, it didn't feel real. The air felt lighter, the world bigger, but I couldn't shake the feeling that the prison walls were still with me.

Lisa stayed behind, and leaving her was one of the hardest things I've ever done. But I knew I had to make it—for both of us.

Adjusting to life outside was harder than I'd imagined. The stigma, the restrictions, the constant fear of failure—it was overwhelming. But I had a plan: stay sober, go to school, and prove to the world—and myself—that I was more than my past.

When Lisa finally joined me on the outside, it was like the missing piece of my life clicked into place. We were both wearing our prison-issued shoes and shorts to school, and it was October in the Pacific Northwest (PNW), still figuring out how to navigate this new world. But we had each other, and that was enough.

Finding Our Place with P2P

Joining P2P was a turning point for us. We were nervous at first—unsure if we belonged in a space filled with people who seemed so polished, so accomplished.

But from the moment we joined, we were welcomed with open arms. P2P wasn't just a program; it was a family. They believed in us, even when we struggled to believe in ourselves.

Through P2P, we found our voices, our purpose, and a community that understood what it meant to fall—and to rise.

Conclusion

Lisa and I often talk about what it means to fall. It's not just about hitting the ground; it's about what you do when you're there.

We've fallen more times than we can count, but every time, we've gotten back up. Not because it was easy, but because it was necessary.

Our journey isn't over. There are still challenges ahead, still moments of doubt and fear. But we face them together, with love in our hearts and hope in our hands.

And if you're reading this, wondering if you can rise after your own fall, let me tell you this: you can. Reach for the hands that reach for you. Trust in your strength. And never, ever stop believing that you are more than your worst moment.

Contraband gifts Lisa and I made as a token of our marriage (June 11, 2021)
Source: Photo by Lisa Guirsch

Wedding flowers in a hopeless place (June 11, 2021)
Source: Photo by Lisa Guirsch

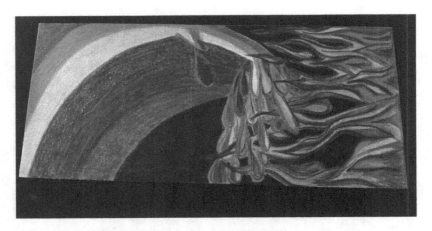

Wedding gift from Rachel to Lisa (June 11, 2021)
Source: Photo by Lisa Guirsch

The first time my mother got to put her arms around me in five years (2022)
Source: Photo by Lisa Guirsch

Lisa and Rachel (November 6, 2023)
Source: Photo by Lisa Guirsch

Rachel picking me up at the gate (CCCF 2022)
Source: Photo by Lisa Guirsch

149

Fallen

Lisa and her mom right before her mom's cancer surgery (WCCW 2016)
Source: Photo by Lisa Guirsch

Lisa and Rachel (December 2022)
Source: Photo by Lisa Guirsch

Rachel and Lisa (2024)
Source: Photo by Lisa Guirsch

Lisa's brother Marty and her baby niece, not very long after Lisa went to prison (2016)
Source: Photo by Lisa Guirsch

Chapter 10

The Wall: Behind and Beyond—The Evolution of Phillip Alvin Jones

By Phillip Alvin Jones

Introduction to Phillip Alvin Jones' Chapter

By Dr. Stanley Andrisse

Phillip Alvin Jones has endured a life journey marked by profound challenges and remarkable resilience. Phillip's path to incarceration was shaped by a confluence of factors including economic hardship, mental health struggles, and the impact of harsh sentencing policies. These drivers illustrate the systemic issues that contribute to high incarceration rates among marginalized communities.

From a young age, Phillip faced the harsh realities of poverty, which often pushes individuals toward survival strategies that conflict with the law. Additionally, the lack of access to adequate mental health care and substance abuse treatment further complicated his circumstances, leading to situations where criminal behavior was more a result of unaddressed needs than intentional wrongdoing. These challenges were compounded by stringent sentencing laws that offered little room for rehabilitation or redemption.

Despite these adversities, Phillip's journey within the criminal legal system is one of profound transformation. Sentenced to

(continued)

(continued)

life in prison at the age of 19, he was thrust into an environment of darkness and dehumanization. Yet, he found solace and strength in the resilience of his spirit. His greatest accomplishment, as he proudly asserts, is maintaining his sanity and humanity in the face of relentless adversity. This resilience is a testament to his determination to rise above the circumstances of his confinement.

The turning point in Phillip's journey came six years into his incarceration, during his time at the Maryland Correctional Adjustment Center, a supermax facility. Isolated and confined for 23 hours a day, Phillip sought refuge in books, immersing himself in the teachings of Malcolm X, Marcus Garvey, and Assata Shakur. These literary mentors provided him with a roadmap to self-empowerment, resilience, and the importance of education.

Phillip's interaction with me and the Prison to Professionals (P2P) program further fueled his transformation. P2P provided him with a sense of identity, dignity, and respect, which were often denied within the prison system. The program's support was instrumental in helping Phillip transcend his circumstances, enabling him to uncover his potential and equipping him with the skills necessary for successful reintegration into society.

Today, Phillip is a testament to the power of personal growth and the human spirit's capacity for resilience. His journey from a fragmented youth to a man committed to continual growth serves as an inspiration to others navigating the complexities of the criminal justice system. Through his story, Phillip Alvin Jones exemplifies the transformative power of education, resilience, and the unwavering belief in one's potential to achieve greatness.

At 19, I was sentenced to life in prison. In the deafening echo of the prison doors, I struggled to comprehend the enormity of my sentence. That moment marked the beginning of a journey—a quest not just for survival but for transformation.

I was once very fragmented, like a puzzle with missing pieces, a young youth lost in the labyrinth of self-discovery. For most of my formative years, I was trapped in a cycle of stagnation, constantly returning to the starting point. My life was an attestation to struggle, yet it is within the struggle that forged a path that led to my transformation and fostered my commitment to continual growth. Embarking on this transformation journey was no effortless task, yet I persisted because I was hungry for a new me.

As an emerging adult lacking parental guidance, I was quickly seduced by the charm of what appeared trendy or "cool," a vulnerability that led me down the wrong path and inevitably to my incarceration at the age of 19. I was found guilty of a crime I committed and sentenced to life in prison, augmented by an additional 20 years. Although my crime was severe, I am thankful that it did not culminate in the loss of a life. Nevertheless, each day I wake up brings with it a stark reminder of the harm I caused, a burden that I am destined to bear until my last breath.

The seriousness of my sentence was something I couldn't fully fathom. At 19, my adolescent brain couldn't grasp the weight of a life sentence. Only later, in the solitude of my cell, did the full reality sink in. The total weight of my situation only struck me once I heard the chilling echo of the prison doors closing in my ears, symbolizing the beginning of my incarceration. Yet, even at that moment, the weight of my sentence was beyond my understanding, and this lack of understanding persisted with me for years.

My awakening came six years into my incarceration as I sat in the confines of the Maryland Correctional Adjustment Center. I was transferred to the supermax facility following my involvement in a riot at the Jessup Correctional Institution, or "The Annex," as it was known. In the solitude of my cell, confined for 23 hours each day, I needed something more than physical exercise to occupy my time. Thus, I turned to books and immersed myself in a diverse range. I devoured the works of Malcolm X, Marcus Garvey, and Assata Shakur, among many others. Malcolm X's teachings instilled an unwavering resilience in me, while Marcus Garvey imparted valuable lessons of self-empowerment, racial pride, and the value of education. Assata Shakur, on the other hand, personifies the daily struggle for freedom, a battle with which I am intimately familiar.

Biographies fascinated me, as their narratives gave me insights, introspection, and personal growth. The knowledge I unearthed during my thirst for knowledge opened up a passport in my mind and illuminated my path toward self-betterment and personal development. During these intellectual ventures, I encountered an axiom that resonated deeply within me and has since become a staple of my existence: "emulate preeminence." But what does it mean to channel greatness? It's the intentional act of seeking inspiration from those exceptional individuals who have achieved extraordinary accomplishments.

This philosophy, in turn, has shaped my guiding ethos. I found myself deeply drawn to the changes that these prolific leaders have achieved through their steadfast commitment and unyielding diligence. I then realized that I, too, could aspire to comparable heights by integrating their methods into my approach. I could elevate myself to similar pinnacles by infusing their strategies into my personal outlook and life perspective. My humble beginnings and the scarcity of resources that characterized my upbringing did not have to be my downfall. Instead, I could adopt the guiding principles of these inspirational figures I had grown to revere, letting their wisdom reshape my perspective of my circumstances.

Before my journey into the world of knowledge, I was a blank slate, bereft of any understanding or context. This lack of awareness was a hindrance, leading to unproductive decisions. However, my most significant revelation was that wisdom is molded by values. As my quest for knowledge progressed, my thought processes and values underwent a positive metamorphosis. I noticed a shift in the way I view things. I would listen to conversations I once agreed with, only to question those viewpoints as backward or simply uninformed over time. This, for me, was the power of knowledge. So, education is not merely the acquisition of facts but a targeted learning experience that hones competencies, further enriching the quality of life. That, my friend, is the transformative journey I have embarked on.

In choosing the path of education, I sought to rise above my circumstances, challenge the narrative of my past, and prove that my ongoing confinement contradicts the essence of justice. I was no longer a threat to society! I had evolved into a distinct individual, far removed from the uninformed, emerging adult who had entered prison 34 years prior. With this new sense of self, I was now inexorably drawn to dissecting the societal conundrums that propel mass incarceration and perpetuate a system that dispenses draconian sentences as if they were mere tokens. This is not simply a contemplation of my circumstances but an urgent call to address the crucial need for reform within our justice system.

Our criminal justice system stands at a crossroads, crying out for comprehensive reform. The path we currently tread cannot be sustained. We need to craft a criminal justice system that epitomizes fairness, precision, second chances, and financial prudence. If we fail to integrate these fundamentals, it's not just the individuals who are incarcerated that lose out, but our society as a whole bears the cost of missed potential.

As a society, our shared duty is to reconcile public safety with the humane treatment of those behind prison bars. Why should we not strive for both in a society that prides itself on civilization? Can we design a system that seeks justice without resorting to revenge? The answer lies within the principles of restorative justice: taking responsibility, demonstrating sincere regret, making restitution, and promoting healing. What objection could there be to investing in such a system?

As a country, we must prioritize the separation of politics from discussions of law enforcement. The politicization of our law enforcement agencies compromises their essential function: safeguarding the citizenry while preserving their rights. Justice is compelled to act with impartiality; without it, we risk allowing subconscious biases to pervade an institution where the principle of fairness is paramount.

But how do we fix our flawed criminal justice system amid a politically charged environment? We must revisit and reassess our beliefs and always seek out better solutions. Reimagining correctional practices is urgent, and as a society, we could also benefit from gleaning insights from our European neighbors globally who emphasize rehabilitation rather than retribution.[1] Most European countries often impose shorter sentences, even for serious crimes,[2] and utilize alternatives like community services, probation, or electronic monitoring. This strategy not only reduces prison overcrowding but also promotes rehabilitation and reintegration. In contrast to the United States, where life sentences without parole are common, most European countries either do not have such sentences or allow for parole eligibility within 20–35 years. Their focus is not on indefinite imprisonment but rather on evaluating an individual's development and potential for reintegration into society.[3] This recommendation is not a dispute of right versus wrong or a critique of the inequities in our existing justice system. Instead, it chronicles the journey of a young man who, despite losing his way, managed to escape the gloom that resulted from a turbulent upbringing.

Lacking the blueprint I needed, I stood firm, unwavering on self-betterment. I rejected the common stereotypes associated with young men of color, aspiring instead to illuminate a path of hope for those who might tread in my footsteps. Stumbling is not to be seen as a disgrace, for we are all prone to falter sometimes. The pursuit of perfection is not the objective; the essence lies in the relentless resilience to rise, dust of the setbacks, and persist until your stride is firm and confident—this path I willingly chose.

Undeniably, there were moments when my circumstances thwarted my progress. Prison is an unrelenting abyss, a place where hope struggles to breathe. I weathered hard nights; however, I refused to allow the cling of the prison gates that closed behind me to echo the final chapter of my story. I vehemently refused to surrender to the notion of dying or spending the rest of my life in prison. I firmly resolved that although my physical being was confined, I would never permit my mind to be imprisoned.

By adhering to this conviction, I persistently sought to expand my knowledge, yearning for growth and enlightenment despite the constraints of my situation. Each day, I would rise with a plan to outshine the previous day, a mantra that has become my hope. I constantly exercise my mind as rigorously as my body. This often meant reaching out beyond the prison walls to external organizations or agencies, seeking involvement in their programs to keep my mind active. As a lifer in prison, immediate access to such programs is not always granted, as they are typically geared toward individuals with an impending release date. However, I adamantly refuse to accept this status quo and allow it to stunt my growth. I was not going to permit my incarceration to strip me of access to opportunities and self-development.

One of the most consequential and transformative programs I managed to partake in was Prison to Professionals, spearheaded by the visionary Dr. Stanley Andrisse, who himself had spent 10 years in prison and was told by his sentencing judge that he would never amount to anything, and yet he proved the judge wrong. Not only did he rise above the stigma of prison, but he also exceeded expectations as an endocrinologist scientist. This is truly an accomplishment that needs to be celebrated. The program catalyzed a change in my thought processes, broadened my horizons, and equipped me with the tools to navigate interactions beyond the prison walls.

Despite my prison confinement, I was never treated as an outsider; rather, I was embraced with a sense of belonging. I am grateful to Dr. Stanley Andrisse and his team for seeing beyond the prison number assigned to me and acknowledging my humanity. I was referred to by my given name, a legacy from my father, a mantle I vowed to honor and uplift. I yearned for our name to signify greatness, to transcend the shadows of addiction and imprisonment that clouded my past. I was intent on rewriting the narrative of my family circumstances. I refused to let my story be reduced to a tale of drug-addicted parents, the tragic loss of two siblings, and a life sentence. I was determined to add more chapters to my life story, chapters filled with hope and resilience. And so, in the face of adversity, I continue to rise.

Today, I am not only Phillip, the incarcerated person; I am Phillip, the author; Phillip, the motivational speaker; Phillip, the entrepreneur; and Phillip, the podcast host. My journey doesn't end here; my list of roles and accomplishments continues to expand. Alongside my daily commitments, I feel it's incumbent upon me to use my voice to highlight the plight of numerous young individuals serving time in prison. They, like myself, made a mistake at an early age and now, as adults, find themselves also incarcerated. Interestingly, many have grown and matured into persons of worth, even within the confines of prison walls, thus making them deserving of a second chance. Are they not redeemable? If tried today, their sentences would likely be significantly less severe than the punishment they've already endured. Why, then, do we overlook this particular demographic?

As a society, our approach toward these individuals needs to be more empathetic. We need to reassess and realign our values, keeping an eye on rehabilitation and reintegration. It necessitates a thorough overhaul and recalibration of our societal values, prioritizing rehabilitation and reintegration. Our eyes must turn to those communities that are underserved and plagued by drug problems. The creation of opportunities within these areas is essential. This action not only aids in reducing crime rates but also paves the way for employment opportunities.

Throughout my 34 years of incarceration, I witnessed countless Black and brown men serving draconian sentences for a single mistake. Many of these men, like me, grew up in neighborhoods plagued by drug addiction and deep poverty. Our everyday lives resembled a torturous labyrinth, filled with unattainable dreams of a brighter future. Unfortunately, we faced the grim reality of either dying young or being sent to prison.

While a few managed to navigate their way out of our communities through athletic prowess, most of us found ourselves tethered by the stringent bonds of poverty—a situation from which we struggled to extricate ourselves. We had no sanctuary, no refuge from our destitution—it followed us, cast its long shadow over all we did. Engulfed by the shadow of impoverishment, our identities bore its indelible mark, a mark that led to two tragic paths: death or incarceration.

My journey led me to prison, sentenced to life, while my siblings met their end on these very streets. Could we have altered our lives, painting a different narrative? This question was an elusive luxury for someone with no positive reference to draw upon. Yet, within me, a glimmer of hope prevailed. I clung to the whisper of a dream that my life would not be defined by death or incarceration. Yet, like countless others from impoverished Black and Brown communities, the disproportionate reality of incarceration became my narrative in this land I call home.

The American criminal justice system is a labyrinthine entity. It is a unique and intentional beast that is unparalleled. This construction of such an extensive and unforgiving criminal legal system is a national issue that, when viewed through the lens of the demographics of those incarcerated, reveals a much larger and more sobering issue. Currently, our nation's prisons and jails house nearly two million individuals, a number that is disproportionately represented by African Americans. This is a grave injustice! The phenomenon of mass incarceration not only unjustly deprives individuals of their freedom, but it also inflicts significant social and economic damage upon individuals, their families, and their communities.

The United States allocates billions of dollars to maintain our criminal justice system, a financial burden that weighs heavily on taxpayers. This calls for a reevaluation and development of more efficient, effective solutions. As an advocate, I consistently highlight the profound importance of second chances, especially for those like me who were sentenced during their formative years. As an incarcerated advocate, I lend my voice to illuminate the stories of both those incarcerated and those who have navigated reentry and the barriers that became impediments to successful reintegration. One of my platforms is my podcast, *The Wall: Behind and Beyond*, which aims to debunk misconceptions, myths, and societal issues surrounding those involved within the criminal justice system.

Through this medium, I conduct weekly interviews with individuals striving to effect change within the criminal justice landscape and allow those impacted to share their narratives. It's also a platform that amplifies the voices silenced by the system, thus turning isolation into connections. Often, my podcast provides the only opportunity for these individuals to tell their stories and reveal the truth about their cases. I also utilize my podcast as a networking tool to stay abreast of pertinent information outside of my present environment, which will eventually help in equipping me with a successful reentry upon my release. Today, *The Wall: Behind and Beyond* has emerged as a profound catalyst in unearthing the ingrained biases within our criminal legal system, shedding light on the disproportionate impact it has on the African American community.

The process of reentry begins on the first day of incarceration. Despite the hardships of prison life, we must find ways to evolve into the best versions of ourselves. The dimensions of our cells need not constrain our growth. Incarcerated individuals, like all of us, are human beings. A criminal record is a tangible entity; our identity, however, is an evolving state of being. We are far more than the dehumanizing label placed upon us. With this understanding, I strive daily to act in a manner that brings me pride.

Throughout my day, I regularly devote much of my time to mentoring the youth I interact with. Seeing them reminds me of my past self, and in advocating for criminal justice reform, I am advocating for a different future for them. I aim to humanize their stories and remind society that these young individuals could be their children, nephews, brothers, uncles, and grandsons. Though we cannot change the past, how we use our present defines our future.

During my incarceration, I authored two books: *Exit 2 Excellence*, a roadmap to successful reintegration, and *Risk 2 Resilience*, a guide dedicated to preventing gang affiliation. I strongly believe these resources, born from my personal journey, offer a viable path to effective rehabilitation and hold immense value for educational institutions, reentry-focused organizations, and our justice system. I firmly believe that disseminating these tools to those in jeopardy could markedly decrease our nation's prison numbers. These resources are of critical importance in communities grappling with gang activity, and poverty, and in schools that are experiencing a high rate of school-to-prison pipeline. These publications provide a roadmap for successful rehabilitation and should be used within schools, reentry organizations, and the court system. As an advocate deeply involved in the criminal legal system, I believe the schools within underserved communities rely too much on suspensions and arrests to handle disciplinary problems instead of focusing on what might be happening with the student.

There should also be programs that focus on preventing gang activities, counseling, and mentorship within the school system rather than perpetuating the prison-to-school pipeline. We must offer more programs and resources within underserved communities specifically designed to address their unique needs. Meeting people where they are is crucial. While education is vital, we must also emphasize practical, common-sense solutions. We must teach our children what actions to take and what to avoid. Simply telling them not to do something isn't enough; we must also recommend alternative paths and walk them through them until they understand. Just saying "don't do this" without offering another solution is ineffective.

Each year, 650,000 men and women nationwide return from prison to their communities. About half of them will return to prison within a matter of years.

A plethora of things can be attributed to the reasons why so many formerly incarcerated individuals return to prison, such as the lack of resources or connections to resources that can aid prosocial integration. There are also many barriers that a formerly incarcerated person faces daily, such as social stigmatization, employment bias, housing bias, and mental and substance abuse issues. As formerly incarcerated individuals return to society, they must be welcomed by a network of support and resources, particularly for those who have been separated from society for an extended period.

The reality of mass incarceration in the United States presents us with a profound and urgent crisis. It is a crisis that we must strive to overcome. We must explore avenues of reform that chip away at the edifice of mass incarceration. This includes the introduction of alternatives to incarceration programs, the removal of rigid mandatory sentences, the institution of sentencing caps, and the endorsement of second-look policies for those who have served over two decades. We need to ensure that sentencing across states reflects the gravity of the crimes committed. This is not merely a policy change, but rather a societal shift toward justice, compassion, and understanding. By doing so, we not only affirm our commitment to fairness and justice but also our belief in the potential for personal growth and redemption.

Reflecting on my younger days, I am guided into a sphere of introspection, pondering the alternative paths my life may have taken had I not found myself incarcerated. Would I still be alive, or would I have inevitably encountered a similar fate as my brothers? Could a different outcome have awaited me, a misdirected young Black boy, had someone taken notice? Why did no adults step forward to secure our well-being? Why was the mantle of responsibility for my siblings' upbringing entrusted to me at the vulnerable age of seven? At that age, the concept of adulthood was beyond my comprehension, yet I did understand, even then, that adults had a duty to protect their children.

It is with regret that I recognize the failure of both my parents and the system: a shared narrative for many young Black boys and girls. I do not seek to excuse my missteps; instead, I consider the potentialities had my circumstances been different. How might my existence have unfolded outside the constraints of these prison walls? This is a question that I, and many others, confront daily. The "what ifs." This is a question that echoes within me, for I am human. Regardless of societal perceptions of those in prison, we are human beings with emotions, often overwhelmed by feelings.

No matter one's abilities, education, or qualifications, life invariably presents situations that prompt these "what ifs." While I am at a place of understanding, I find that from time to time, my mind will persistently return to this question. As long as I remain incarcerated, there will constantly be a void in my life, prompting me to question what my existence might have been had I not gone to prison. Conversely, as I ponder the "what ifs" that shadow my past, I also question the path ahead. How do I see my future self? I see myself unchained, stepping beyond the confines of these prison walls. I imagine inhaling the fresh air of the outside world, a stark contrast to the oppressive air that permeates the inside of prison. I dream of the precious and joyful moments I will spend with my daughters. I envision myself building a legacy, a beacon of hope for youths who have lost their way. I will share my story and urge them to reach for the stars and immerse themselves in the world of education, for it can alter their life's trajectory. I will plead with them not to bow down to the pressures of the crowd, for such surrender can lead to consequences from which they may never recover.

My story will echo across the world. With this unwavering determination, I face each day. My destiny is not confined to this prison; I am more than my mistakes. I believe God has a plan that awaits me, which may seem a distant dream to those who view life through a static lens. Yet, I see beyond the present, for my current circumstances do not define me.

Like the mythical phoenix, I will rise from the ashes of my past, reborn through incarceration. As I draw near this chapter's end, I choose to impart some wisdom to the youthful version of myself.

As I pen this reflection, I am drawn to the wisdom I wish I could have shared with my younger self, the child who has weathered a storm of life's trials. Phillip, my deepest regrets for the hardship life imposed upon you, for the stolen innocence that comes with a childhood burdened by such immense responsibility. At the tender age of seven, you were unexpectedly thrust into the caretaker role for your younger siblings, a role you didn't ask for yet assumed with a profound sense of duty. Despite your youth, you perceived the absence in your life and courageously stepped into the void. You led not with knowledge but with the wisdom of your heart. You understood the sting of hunger, so you ensured your brothers were fed even when you went without. You knew the ache of solitude, so you ensured they were never alone. You soothed their tears in the absence of your parents while your own heart was quietly breaking.

The day you were sentenced to life in prison was a harsh blow, a transition from one harsh world into another that was even more unforgiving. Yet, in this harsh reality, your concern remained steadfast with your brothers. I comprehend the magnitude of this burden for you. Had you been armed with the knowledge you now have, I am certain that your resilient spirit would have fostered a better life, given the opportunity.

As your older self, I am filled with pride for your journey and the milestones you've achieved in such a harsh environment called prison. Your acceptance of responsibility for the crime you committed is a testament to your character. I see your continuous efforts to make amends and acknowledge your commitment to personal growth. Life will continue to present painful moments that feel like seismic shifts within your heart. In these moments, maintain your focus. Do not allow the pain to derail you from your path of redemption.

Believe in the presence of guardian angels watching over you. Recognize these angels in the individuals you meet along your journey. Some will accompany you for a brief time, others for extended periods. They are there for a season, and when that season concludes, they will depart. Embrace their departure without resentment, for they were there to fulfill a purpose, and once that purpose is completed, it's appropriate to let them go. Phillip, your older self applauds you, for I see the greatness ahead of you. I look forward to a future where we continue to grow, learn, and, most importantly, not let our past define us.

Phillip Alvin Jones, c. 2024

Chapter 11

A Stage Worthy of Freedom

By William Freeman III

Introduction to William Freeman's Chapter

By Dr. Stanley Andrisse

William Freeman III entered the Prison to Professionals (P2P) office in Touchpoint Mondawmin on a cool autumn day in 2019, the air crisp with the season's change, and the weight of systemic inequities trailing him like a shadow. Mondawmin Mall is in west Baltimore, the backdrop of "The Wire" and blocks away from where Freddie Gray lay lifeless. William carried a story that was all too familiar yet uniquely his own—a story of surviving and resisting the structural forces designed to keep him in place.

He sat across from me, his gaze steady but filled with the resolve of someone who had defied the odds. "Dr. Stan," he began, his voice unwavering, "statistically, I shouldn't be here. The system isn't built for people like me to succeed after a criminal conviction like the one I have. But here I am."

I nodded, acknowledging the truth of his statement. The criminal legal system is riddled with disparities—racial, educational, and economic—that disproportionately impact Black communities like ours in Baltimore. William had faced those barriers head-on and refused to be defined by them.

(continued)

(continued)

"What accomplishment are you most proud of since your interaction with the system?" I asked in a later conversation, knowing the depth of the question.

He took a moment and then replied, "I'm most proud of defying the expectations society placed on me. P2P introduced me to a network of changemakers who helped me push beyond the generational norms of degradation. It was through these connections that I found a sustainable path forward."

I remembered his journey vividly. He brought up the time I sat on the advisory board for the Education Trust National. "You recused yourself from deciding on my application for the Justice Fellows Policy Program," he recalled, "but when asked, you vouched for me. You said, 'He's a powerful speaker who knows higher-ed policy!' That moment was a turning point for me. I was chosen, and that opened the door to a sustainable career at ETN."

I could see how much that experience meant to him. His ability to navigate and transform his narrative was precisely why I had advocated for him. His voice, his knowledge, and his passion for educational equity were too valuable to be ignored.

"And P2P?" I prompted, curious about the role our program had played in his journey.

"P2P was life-changing," he said. "It wasn't just about resources; it was about breaking down barriers and creating opportunities. The network you built gave me the tools to challenge the systems that sought to limit me. It gave me the confidence to thrive in spaces that were never meant for me."

William's story is a testament to resistance, to the power of community, and to the necessity of dismantling the structures that perpetuate inequality. He isn't just surviving; he's reshaping the narrative, proving that liberation and success are possible, even in the face of systemic oppression.

In August 2018, I sat to the right of my attorney, behind a heavy oak table. Behind us, a chorus of opposition to my early release, shadowed our appeal. A heavy silence was broken only by the shuffle of papers, an occasional whisper at my back of subtle commands to keep my hands on the table, and the distant hum of an old air conditioner. Judge Charles Peters scanned the courtroom before glaring in my direction. He peeked over his glasses, clinging to the edge of his nose. It was clear he was wrestling with his decision that ultimately would be contrary to what the state's attorney wanted: denial. After several trips ordering me back to the concrete bullpen located in the basement of the courthouse, he declared, "Mr. Freeman, I am releasing you to finish your education and do all of the things you otherwise would not be able to do in prison." At that moment, a whirlwind of emotions surged through me—relief, disbelief, and a cautious hope. The weight of the past 21 years had momentarily lifted, replaced by the reality of freedom that seemed more dangerous than the prison setting I grew to believe was normal. I owed society but first I would need to take my place in a world that had once deemed me irreparable.

This was not merely a directive; it was a call to action, a defining moment that set the tone for the arduous but rewarding journey ahead. That moment marked a pivotal turning point in my life, one where the trajectory of my existence shifted from confinement to possibility. My educational journey evolved from a desolate consequence to a vivid scene of transformation, each step displaying how the unshackling of freedom, paired with a network of support, could rewrite a life's narrative.

As an incarcerated student, I often reflected on the narrative I held against standardized education. I questioned its role in upholding societal structures, including the valorization of militaristic conquest, the justification of eminent domain, and the myth of meritocracy as a fair playing field. My intellectual awakening began behind bars, but the education that Goucher College brought inside the prison was now set in motion. Goucher professors had written to the court highlighting my education inside, my academic potential.

Society has made it easier for me to go to prison than to go to college.

Life after a felony conviction felt like uncharted territory. January 25, 2019, the first day I set foot on Goucher College's main campus, felt like stepping onto a stage to audition where every movement was scrutinized and every word weighed. My heart raced, not from exertion but from the weight of possibility, and I knew at that moment that this was no ordinary day, it was the beginning of a performance worthy of an Oscar.

When I first drove northbound on 695 en route to Goucher College, it had been more than 20 years since I had been behind the wheel of a car. The freedom of the open road felt surreal. As I approached the campus, I felt a mixture of anticipation and trepidation. It was a stage of my life worthy of freedom, but it came without a script. Back then, my existence unfolded more adlibbed than scripted. Like a rapper in the booth crafting verses on the spot, I faced the open road and the uncharted world of academia with raw improvisation. Each turn of the wheel and every step on Goucher's campus felt like freestyling through a life that demanded reinvention, with no map or manual to guide me.

Freedom: A Double-Edged Sword

Freedom, in its purest form, is a chance—nothing more, nothing less. But it did not shield me from the pains of reentry or the challenges of navigating a world that often judges those with an imperfect background. Goucher College introduced me to the safety of a world apart from the one I once considered normal. That safety was known as the infamous "Goucher Bubble"—as it was often called—was both real and metaphorical. It represented a space where privilege and intellectual exploration thrived, but also a place in proximity to the city of Baltimore where my insecurities and doubts were magnified.

I drove slowly up to the guard station, my mind raced with doubt, my pulse quickening as the cool air prickled against my perspiring skin. The faint rustle of leaves on the campus trees contrasted sharply with the weight of unease pressing on my chest. "What if he calls me back?" I thought, imagining the guard's voice cutting through the quiet. My grip on the steering wheel moments earlier lingered as a phantom tension in my hands that felt all too familiar. At 5 mph, I eased toward the unknown feeling like a test, the whisper of my breath the only sound breaking the silence of my apprehension. Would the guard suddenly realize my background and rescind his decision to let me in? "Surely he missed something," I mumbled, replaying our brief exchange, sneaking a view of him in the rearview mirror. The questions he asked did not seem designed to uncover secrets, but I answered cautiously, improvising except when he asked my name.

"Freeman! William Freeman!" I stated, the name leaving my lips with a weight I hadn't anticipated. For so long, my name had been reduced to a number—State Identification Number 1785558. That DOC-assigned identifier was my identity for 7,670 days. Handing over my license to confirm I was, in fact, a "free man," I could not help but flash back to another checkpoint, another gate. I saw myself standing outside the bubble of housing unit C at the Maryland Correctional Institution in Jessup (MCI-J), waiting for an officer to hand me a green pass granting permission to move beyond the unit.

The world, it seemed, had always been a stage. In prison, my performance was survival—projecting strength when I felt vulnerable, carefully selecting words to navigate the politics of the yard, and masking uncertainty behind a stoic facade during parole hearings. In classrooms, I rehearsed confidence, even as imposter syndrome whispered that I did not belong. The stage shifted, but the performance endured. At Goucher, that act expanded—answering questions in seminars with the poise of someone who had spent years studying, even if I had only recently learned the material. Every raised hand, every presentation, became a scene in a larger production of belonging and self-reclamation. But now, it demanded a performance worthy of Denzel Washington. My past was a history book I no longer cared to reread—it owed me nothing. My future, however, was a blank script waiting to be written. And I was determined to be both the writer and lead actor.

The Performance of Belonging

Navigating life on Goucher's campus often felt like an audition for a role I was not sure I could play convincingly. I remember standing outside my first classroom, rehearsing my introduction silently, afraid that any misstep would expose me. In seminar discussions, I carefully measured each word, listening twice as much as I spoke, hoping my insights would match the polished contributions of my peers. Walking across the quad, I felt the weight of invisible eyes, as if the campus itself questioned my right to be there. Every interaction felt like a scene, and I was determined to at least practice relentlessly and to walk in the role of a nontraditional student traditionally, even when doubt gnawed at me.

Justice-impacted students are expected to participate and at least master the role of being a student. I recall the first time I raised my hand during a seminar discussion. My palms were clammy, and I rehearsed my response in my head multiple times before daring to speak. When I finally voiced my thoughts, I felt as though the entire class had turned to analyze not just my answer, but my very presence. In moments like these I was frequently nodding along in agreement even when I did not fully grasp the reading, carefully mirroring the academic language used by peers to avoid drawing attention to the gaps in my knowledge. Each of these small performances built a shield between me and the stigma I feared would surface if anyone knew the full extent of my background. This performative aspect reflects the complex intersection of identity, perception, and systemic inequality.

My initial days at Goucher were marked by internal battles. Would my classmates see through my facade? Would the professors notice my hesitations when referencing books what certain academic concepts? In those moments, I relied on my mother's advice: "Act like you belong, and no one will question your presence."

The campus itself was a paradox. Its tall greenery and sprawling grounds made it appear both impenetrable and inviting. It was January 2019. The crisp air carried no hint of Baltimore City's grit. This was not just a campus to me; it was a proving ground. Judge Charles Peters had given me a singular directive when he ordered me to Gaudenzia's Drug Treatment Facility in Annapolis, Maryland: "Finish your degree, Mr. Freeman."

Here I was, crossing into a world where my past would either dissolve in shadows or loom over me like a specter. Either way, I was ready to perform.

Building the Foundation at Goucher College

Less than 90 days removed from prison, I found myself seated next to Betsy DeVos at a roundtable discussion. The Vera Institute of Justice had convened a series of meetings on Capitol Hill for corrections officials, college faculty, and formerly incarcerated students. I was asked to share my experiences as a student transitioning from incarceration to higher education. As I sat alongside leaders in the field, I recounted the challenges of adapting to campus life, navigating stigma, and advocating for support systems that were often lacking.

The room felt heavy with the weight of expectation, but I knew my voice represented countless others who had yet to step foot into these academic spaces. Eleven of the fourteen programs represented were part of the U.S. Department of Education's Second Chance Pell (SCP) Experimental Sites Initiative, including the Goucher Prison Education Partnership (GPEP).

GPEP was more than just an academic program for me; it was a lifeline. Amy Roza, the executive director at the time, consistently emphasized GPEP's mission: to deliver quality education that could empower returning citizens to compete in society. The classes were rigorous and eye-opening. In one seminar, Masculinities, the professor encouraged us to explore connections between our experiences and the frameworks introduced by R.W. Connell. Learning that the author had transitioned their gender challenged societal norms about identity and masculinity. It forced me to confront my understanding of what it meant to be a man, a student, and a formerly incarcerated individual.

Finding My Tribe

While GPEP offered unparalleled academic preparation, it lacked the community networks necessary for full reintegration. I knew I wanted to teach one day, but I had no one in my network who shared my unique experiences. Enter Prison to Professionals (P2P). P2P became the conduit connecting justice-impacted academics across the United States. Through P2P, I found individuals who understood my journey—people who had walked similar paths and were willing to share their insights. One interaction stands out vividly. During a virtual P2P meeting, I shared the frustration I felt after being overlooked for a leadership role on campus. A fellow member, who had also faced rejection after incarceration, shared how they leveraged rejection into an opportunity to build a mentorship initiative for justice-impacted students. Their resilience inspired me to shift my perspective. Instead of internalizing setbacks, I began developing workshops focused on public speaking and self-advocacy for other returning citizens.

This community reminded me that I was not alone. They gave me the language to advocate for myself, the tools to navigate stigma, and the sense of belonging I had long been searching for. Each interaction reinforced that belonging is not about perfection is about showing up authentically and supporting others on their journeys. These relationships helped me turn the performance of belonging into something more authentic.

Transitioning to Johns Hopkins

The move to Johns Hopkins Bloomberg School of Public Health was both transformative and challenging. Alienation and imposter syndrome were constant companions. I recall sitting in a seminar on public health policy, gripping my pen tightly as if it could anchor me in the swirling sea of academic jargon. The professor's question hung in the air, and one by one, students eagerly jumped in with references to internships at think tanks and summer research programs at prestigious universities. I shifted in my seat, feeling the weight of every year I had spent behind bars.

A student beside me turned and casually asked, "Where did you go for your undergrad studies?"

My throat tightened. "Goucher College," I replied, keeping it brief, hoping the conversation would end there. But their curiosity lingered, and I felt exposed.

Internally, I rehearsed what I could say the next time without bearing my soul. Socially, I often navigated a cultural chasm, nodding along during conversations about gap years in Europe or dorm life—experiences that underscored the years I had spent in confinement.

As class ended, I packed my bag slowly, watching my peers filter out, laughing, and planning study sessions. The loneliness settled in like a familiar shadow, but I reminded myself why I was there. Each seminar, even with its discomfort, was another step toward reclaiming the education I had once thought impossible.

Mentors and allies at Hopkins played a pivotal role. They validated my voice and experiences, helping me recognize that my lived experiences offered unique insights into public health disparities and social justice issues. This support eroded the isolation I initially felt and allowed me to embrace authenticity over performance.

Bridging Individual and Collective Identity

My involvement with P2P was the zenith of my journey toward integrating individual and collective identity. One event stands out—a national conference on reentry and higher education where I was invited to present. Standing before a room filled with policymakers, educators, and formerly incarcerated students, I shared how P2P not only bridged gaps in academic access but also fostered community resilience. After the session, a young man approached me, sharing that my story had inspired him to apply for college despite his doubts. That single interaction crystallized the power of collective identity, each of us carrying the torch for others who were still finding their way. This community celebrated authenticity and provided a foundation of trust and mutual understanding. Through this integration, I began to see my story as part of a broader tapestry of resilience and transformation.

The journey from incarceration to higher education taught me that reintegration is not a solitary endeavor. For institutions, the lesson is clear—justice-impacted students need more than just coursework; they need communities that foster belonging and resilience. Academic institutions must develop comprehensive support systems that extend beyond the classroom, addressing both social and psychological barriers to reintegration. A strong network of mentors, peer groups, and accessible resources can transform lives, bridging the gap between potential and achievement.

For students navigating similar paths, the most valuable lesson I learned was to seek out those who understand the weight of your journey. Authenticity, once perceived as a vulnerability, became my greatest strength when shared in the right spaces. The connections I formed through programs like Prison to Professionals (P2P) reminded me that isolation is not a requirement of reintegration—community is.

I recall one evening, sitting across from a fellow P2P member after a workshop. We talked long after the session ended, sharing stories of rejection and triumph. His words stayed with me: "Your past doesn't define your future, but it will shape how you lead others." That conversation reinforced the importance of mentorship and solidarity. It reminded me that while the road ahead might be uncertain, walking it alongside others makes the journey more bearable—and, often, more transformative.

For justice-impacted students, I say this: Seek out those who see your potential, not your past. Let the weight of your experiences fuel your growth and remember that every step forward is a victory not just for yourself, but for everyone watching and waiting for their turn.

Conclusion: A Call to Action

I remember walking from the Dorsey Building, where the President of Goucher College is located, down a light gray brick path. Although I was no stranger to the pathway between Dorsey and the lawn by the Athenaeum—home to the library and student store—and student housing, I had never considered how that path would one day lead me to the stage where I would deliver the commencement speech. The fact that the committee chose me to address the entire Goucher community as the student representative—on the heels of George Floyd's assassination, at a time when America was forced to reckon with the fragility of nonwhite life—was profound.

As I spoke, I caught glimpses of nodding heads and encouraging smiles. Yet, I felt indifferent toward those smiling faces, overrun by emotion and the need to resist the fear that swirled in my gut. This was my moment to merge the education I had gained before enrolling in Goucher with the formal education I completed at the conclusion of my coursework. My eyes filled with tears, blinding me from reading my speech word for word, so I continued speaking from the heart. As I finished, I feared I had lived up to the "angry Black man" stereotype. But then, I paused and witnessed a sea of onlookers rise to their feet, erupting into a standing ovation.

At that moment, I realized I was no longer performing. I was living my truth, sharing not just knowledge but pieces of the person I had become. Education played a vital role in creating neutral grounds for an unlikely encounter. Those whose family lineage includes access to higher education can only imagine what it means to disrupt an inheritance of exclusion from equitable post-secondary opportunities. Individuals do not create themselves; they are shaped by the totality of their experiences.

I received my bachelor's degree in my left hand while shaking hands with the college president, losing sight of all the obstacles ahead. In the words of W.E.B. Du Bois, "The Negro freedom was like a moment in the sun." Du Bois was writing about Black people's emancipation from chattel slavery, yet in many ways, mass incarceration in the 21st century mirrors those injustices. However, at the very least, learning to read is no longer a crime punishable by death.

Walking back to my seat to the sound of applause ringing in my ears felt like the closing act of one performance and the opening scene of another, with the promise of more to follow. I had earned the credential that so many who remain paralyzed below the poverty line have been denied. Yet, the greater challenge ahead was to find employment where decision-makers committed to long-term investments in justice-impacted individuals.

To institutions, policymakers, and individuals alike, the call is clear: invest in the lives of justice-impacted students, academics, and early-career professionals with the same commitment afforded to traditional college graduates. Dedicate resources to their professional development. A college degree, in itself, does not guarantee workforce readiness—those skills must be learned. Instead, higher education prepares individuals to ask the right questions when faced with uncertainty, to collaborate with those who are different from them, and to embrace constructive criticism with the understanding that change is inevitable.

When we create pathways to education and opportunity, we effect change that extends beyond the individual student—we uplift entire communities. Millions of Americans are directly affected by incarceration through their family connections. Studies show that half of the U.S. population has a close family member who has been incarcerated. Additionally, one in five people has experienced the incarceration of a parent, and approximately 2.6 million children currently have a parent serving time in prison. These statistics underscore the widespread and generational impact of the criminal justice system, highlighting the urgency of addressing these challenges through education, advocacy, and community support.

The stage is set. Now is the time to act.

William Freeman III author photo

Keynote at the 11th National Conference for Higher Education in Prison, c. November 2021

Roundtable at Capitol Hill with Betsy Devos, c. 2019
Source: Photo by William G. Freeman III

William Freeman III author photo

183

A Stage Worthy of Freedom

Commencement Speech at his graduation, Goucher College Commencement, May 2022
Source: Photo by William G. Freeman III

P2P "We Are The Experts" film interview, c. 2019

184

Breaking Chains, Building Futures

Commencement speech at Lane, c. January 2022
Source: Photo by William G. Freeman III

Chapter 12

The Long Road Home

By Mancy Thompson

Introduction to Mancy Thompson's Chapter
By Dr. Stanley Andrisse

The Struggle for Redemption in a System of Injustice

There is a pervasive myth in America—that those who are incarcerated have somehow forfeited their right to dignity, to redemption, and to a future that isn't defined by their past. It is a myth built on centuries of systemic racism, economic exploitation, and a criminal justice system that profits from the misery of those it imprisons.

Mass incarceration in this country is not just a problem; it is a crisis. As of 2023, more than two million people are locked behind bars in the United States, and nearly seven million are under some form of correctional control—whether in prison, jail, or on probation or parole. The United States has the highest incarceration rate in the world, a disturbing statistic that disproportionately affects Black and brown communities. More than

(continued)

(continued)

1 in 3 Black boys born today will be sentenced to prison, and in some states, the majority of Black men will be incarcerated at some point in their lives. These figures are not just numbers; they are the lived experiences of people like Mancy Thompson, whose journey from the battlefield to the prison yard and, finally, to a place of redemption embodies the struggle of many who have been pushed to the margins by a society that profits from their incarceration.

I first met Mancy Thompson in 2017, when he walked into my life—like so many others in our communities—bearing the scars of a system that had failed him. But unlike many, Mancy came with a quiet determination, a will to rise above the labels and limitations imposed on him. He had been through the fires of war and the brutalities of prison, but the man who sat before me was not defeated. Mancy's story isn't just about his survival; it's about his transformation—and it's a story that needs to be told.

Mancy's path to redemption did not come without struggle. It came with hardship, yes. But it also came with support, community, and the unwavering belief that his past did not have to define his future. His story is the story of many individuals who enter the prison system and are left to rot in a system that offers no hope, no opportunity for rehabilitation, and no real chance for change. It is the story of a man who found his way back, not just to himself but to a life of service, giving back to those who were once in his shoes.

The odds were stacked against him. Prison sentences, often fueled by the War on Drugs, are disproportionately handed down to Black and brown individuals. A staggering 64% of people incarcerated in the United States have a high school diploma or less, and many, like Mancy, find themselves caught in a cycle of violence, trauma, and despair. The trauma inflicted by incarceration—physical, psychological, emotional—is undeniable. Yet, within that system, there exists the potential for change. And Mancy Thompson is a testament to that.

From his time in the Marine Corps to his years behind bars, Mancy's life has been marked by both violence and resilience. Yet, when he walked into my office, he didn't see himself as a product of the system. He saw himself as someone capable of something greater. This chapter is a window into that transformation—a story of redemption, not just for Mancy, but for the millions who are still locked away, forgotten by society.

Mancy's journey was not his alone to walk. It was a collective effort, one rooted in the power of community. Through Prison to Professionals (P2P), Mancy found a space where his experiences weren't just acknowledged but valued. He found a place where he could begin the process of healing—not just for himself, but for others who were on the same path. P2P is more than an organization; it is a movement, one that pushes back against a system designed to imprison bodies and minds. Through our work together, I witnessed the healing power of opportunity—the power to change lives, to restore dignity, and to give individuals the tools they need to reclaim their future.

In the pages that follow, you'll read Mancy's story. A story that, like the stories of so many others, is marked by struggle, resilience, and ultimately, hope. It is a story that reminds us all of the truth that the system is not broken—it was designed this way. But as Mancy's journey shows us, the system does not have the final say. The human spirit does.

The Long Road Home

Beginnings: From Baltimore to the Barracks

Growing up in Baltimore, Maryland, life didn't offer much in the way of promise. The city, steeped in history and burdened by its struggles, was both my playground and my prison. My parents separated when I was young, leaving me to navigate a world that seemed determined to hold me down. Baltimore didn't whisper dreams—it shouted survival. The corners were tough, the people tougher, and every day felt like a battle just to stay afloat.

I remember standing on the stoop of our rowhouse, watching the world go by, thinking there had to be more than this. The Marine Corps seemed like my ticket out—a chance to escape the cycle of poverty and violence, to serve, and maybe, just maybe, to see a world beyond West Baltimore's narrow streets.

I signed up with a heart full of hope and resolve, ready to leave behind the only life I'd known. But the journey ahead was far more harrowing than I could have imagined. The year was 1983, and while the Iranian hostage crisis had ended, the world teetered on the edge of new conflicts. My first post was Iceland—a place as cold and distant as the racial tensions simmering beneath the surface. They called us "dark green" Marines, a label meant to unify, but all it did was highlight the divisions. Brotherhood, they said. Yet, inequality found a way to thrive, even in uniform.

From Iceland, I was shipped to Kaneohe, Hawaii—a paradise with a dark undercurrent. In Beirut, the Lebanese Civil War raged, and we were thrust into the heart of the storm. I'll never forget October 1983. A terrorist drove a truck laden with explosives into our barracks. In an instant, 241 of my comrades were gone. I survived, but survival didn't feel like victory. It felt like a burden—a curse that would haunt me for years.

Broken by the Battlefield

I came back from Beirut a changed man. The trauma didn't just scar my body; it fractured my soul. Back then, no one talked about PTSD. They called it "shell shock" or "battle fatigue," but those were just words. The reality was a rage that burned inside me, an isolation that grew with each passing day. My world tilted, and I couldn't find solid ground.

My marriage was crumbling, another casualty of the man I'd become. My wife, who worked for the FBI, saw it before I did. "You're not the same," she said, her voice filled with worry and love. "You need help." But I wasn't ready to hear it. Promotions and bonuses dangled in front of me like carrots on a stick, and I stayed, clinging to the structure of the Corps, hoping it could save me.

It didn't.

The Incident

One night, after another grueling day, I found myself at a bar off base with some friends. We were just trying to unwind, but the air was thick with tension. Words flew, tempers flared, and before long, we were shouting. The line between words and violence blurred, and in the chaos, guns were drawn.

In the heat of the moment, a civilian was killed. I was the one who pulled the trigger. The world seemed to slow, the noise fading into silence. I returned to base that night, clinging to routine, as if it could erase what had happened. But reality was waiting. By dawn, a civilian cop had pieced it together, and I found myself in handcuffs. The Corps couldn't protect me now.

Years Behind Bars

Prison wasn't new to me—I'd danced on the edge before—but this time was different. I wasn't a Marine anymore; I was an inmate, another number in the system. For 23 and a half years, I wrestled with the weight of my actions and the ghosts of Beirut. The violence didn't stop behind bars. Charged with another homicide while incarcerated, I fought every day to survive. It was a brutal world, but even there, I found moments of light.

My military discipline became my lifeline, helping me navigate the chaos of the prison yard. I clung to it like a drowning man to a raft, hoping it would carry me through the storm.

A New Chapter: Coming Home

In 2011, after five parole hearings, I was granted release. Stepping into a world that had moved on without me was jarring. My wife, ever loyal, had relocated to California, and we began to rebuild our lives in Lemon Grove. But the challenges were immense. I was a 50-year-old man with little civilian experience. The job market was brutal, and my past was a constant shadow.

A Second Chance with P2P

In 2015, I returned to Maryland and met Dr. Stanley Andrisse during the Ban the Box campaign. That meeting changed my life. "You've got potential," he said, his eyes filled with conviction. "We can help you find your path." I joined the P2P Scholars Program in 2018, finding a community that believed in my potential and gave me the tools to rebuild my life.

By 2021, I was the program director, using my experiences to guide others. Every day, I worked to show justice-impacted individuals that their past didn't have to define their future. It was hard work, but it was work worth doing.

Looking Ahead

My story is one of resilience and redemption. From the battlefields of Beirut to the prison yards of California, I've walked a long, hard road. But I've found my way to a life of purpose. At P2P, I help others see that they too can rise above their past. The road isn't easy, but it's worth walking.

Dedication

This chapter is dedicated to the memory of my comrades lost in Beirut and to all those who never got the chance to start over. Their stories fuel my mission, reminding me every day why second chances matter.

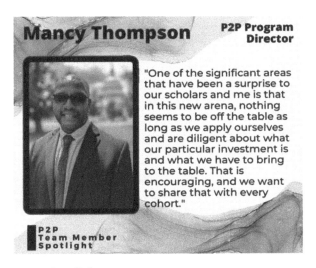

Mancy Thompson Spotlight
Source: Photo by Mancy Thompson

Conclusion: Systemic Injustice, Personal Transformation, and the Path Toward Change

As we close this compilation of stories from the Prison to Professionals (P2P) program, it's clear that the journey from incarceration to empowerment is one shaped not only by individual resilience but by the deep and pervasive systems of inequality that influence every aspect of life for justice-impacted individuals. From the outset, the book sets the stage by exploring the broad systemic drivers of incarceration. Authors such as Oswald Newbold II lay bare the socioeconomic and political forces that continue to disproportionately affect people of color, emphasizing the cycle of poverty, racial and ethnic disparities, and harsh sentencing policies as the foundational pillars of mass incarceration. As Newbold points out, "Structural racism is not just a problem in the criminal justice system; it is the bedrock upon which the system was built." These systems are not accidental—they are intentional structures designed to maintain power imbalances, perpetuate inequality, and trap the most vulnerable members of society in cycles of criminalization.

Building on this foundation, Tenaj Moody highlights how the criminalization of poverty and survivors, particularly those who experience gendered violence, further exacerbates the impact of systemic injustice. Moody brings an intersectional lens to the conversation, illustrating how the systems of incarceration disproportionately affect women, particularly those who are survivors of domestic and sexual violence. As she argues, "The violence we endure does not end with our victimization. The criminal justice system too often becomes the next perpetrator of harm." This narrative extends seamlessly into the reflections of Dr. Brian Metcalf, who underscores the often-overlooked barriers faced by those on the fringes of society, and Judith Negron, who discusses the connection between mental health, education inequity, and the lack of rehabilitative services in prisons. Together, these chapters provide a sobering but necessary examination of how systemic failings—such as underfunded schools, lack of access to mental health care, and inadequate rehabilitation programs—fuel cycles of incarceration.

Transitioning from these macro-level analyses, the personal stories shared by the authors offer powerful testimonies of resilience in the face of these systemic barriers. Dr. Tommy Everette Moore's narrative is one of transformation, emphasizing the role of education and mentorship in helping individuals reclaim their agency and change the course of their lives. His story is a testament to the power of self-determination and support networks, showing that resilience is not merely an internal quality but a collective force. Desiree Riley complements this message, offering a poignant personal account that weaves together themes of poverty, mental health, and the criminalization of poverty. Her experiences highlight how pervasive societal issues manifest in the lives of incarcerated individuals, and the deep internal work necessary to heal and rise above these circumstances.

Dr. Kelsie Becklin expands on these themes, addressing the ways in which mental health issues are criminalized rather than treated, further entrenching marginalized individuals in the justice system. Her insights connect with Elhadji Ndiaye's exploration of the role poverty plays in perpetuating cycles of incarceration, which is a theme we see again in Rachel and Lisa Guirsch's work on the intersection of mental health, harsh sentencing policies, and the over-policing of communities. The contributions of these authors remind us that systemic issues such as over-policing and the criminalization of mental health are not isolated problems—they are interconnected crises that demand comprehensive, integrated solutions.

As we shift toward solutions, the narratives of William Freeman III and Mancy Thompson exemplify the potential for transformation when we invest in education and rehabilitation. Freeman's experience, particularly through his work with the Goucher Prison Education Partnership, illuminates the transformative power of education, not just as a tool for personal development but as a vehicle for systemic change. He argues that "Education is not just about knowledge—it's about survival." Freeman's advocacy for increased access to higher education in prison is a call to action that reverberates throughout this book. Mancy Thompson's contribution further supports this, offering insights into mentorship as a catalyst for healing and empowerment. His work with P2P underscores the critical need for supportive, structured programs that guide individuals through the complex journey of reentry.

This book has taken us on a journey from the structural issues that form the foundation of mass incarceration to the personal narratives of resilience, self-discovery, and transformation. It leaves us with a clear understanding that while the systems that contribute to incarceration are vast and entrenched, there are pathways to change—pathways that are forged through education, mentorship, and a collective commitment to justice. As we move forward, we must recognize that dismantling the prison-industrial complex requires more than just reforming the system—it requires a radical reimagining of justice, one that values healing, rehabilitation, and the human potential for growth.

In closing, we echo the words of Bryan Stevenson, founder of the Equal Justice Initiative, "The opposite of poverty is not wealth; the opposite of poverty is justice." This book is a testament to that truth—reminding us that the fight for justice is ongoing and that through the stories of resilience and transformation, we can begin to build a future where incarceration is no longer the default response to human struggle, but a last resort in a society committed to healing and redemption.

The Hero Within: Empowering the P2P Scholars to Transform Their Lives

As I reflect on the journey of P2P and its transformative power, I am reminded of the lessons in humility, empathy, and the undeniable strength that lies within each of us. Like the characters in the Justice League, each individual who has come through the P2P Scholars Program is a hero in their own right. And yet, just as with the Justice League, these heroes did not emerge out of nowhere; they were nurtured, shaped, and empowered by a force that believed in their potential even when society refused to see it.

Much like the X-Men, those in the P2P community share an undeniable bond—a bond rooted in struggle, in society's rejection, and in the shared experience of being seen as outsiders. But just as Professor X (Charles Xavier) guided his students to hone their unique abilities, so too did I, Professor Andrisse, step into the role of mentor, guiding these, if I may, A-Men and A-Women toward realizing their full potential. In this analogy, the A-Men, our P2P Scholars, and the authors of this book, are not a symbol of superiority or exceptionalism; they are simply a testament to what can happen when society offers its most marginalized a chance to thrive.

We do not claim to be the best; we are not above anyone else. We are simply a living example of the possibility that exists when we stop pretending that people who have been touched by incarceration are broken or lost. In fact, they are not so different from the heroes we read about in comic books. Like those heroes, their strength lies in their unique experiences and the courage they summon to transform them into something powerful, something that can save lives—not only their own, but those of others who find themselves struggling under similar burdens.

The A-Men and A-Women are not just symbols of success—they are a reflection of resilience, determination, and the undeniable truth that anyone, regardless of their past, has the capacity to be a hero. Their stories remind us that heroism is not born in the absence of struggle, but in the willingness to rise above it. And in this way, the A-Men are not so different from the rest of us. They are the embodiment of all that is possible when we offer empathy, authenticity, and support to those who need it most.

In the end, P2P is not about showcasing individual achievement; it's about illustrating a collective truth: that anyone can be a hero when given the opportunity. Through mentorship, through guidance, and through the recognition of the unique value each person brings, we can transform not just the lives of individuals, but entire communities, and ultimately, the very fabric of society itself.

So, as we look at these P2P Scholars, we must remember that they represent not just a few individuals, but the untapped potential within all of us. The story of P2P is not just a story of success; it is a call to action—an invitation to believe in people, to invest in them, and to recognize that in doing so, we are all lifting one another up, one hero at a time.

This, then, is our collective mission: to continue to create space for heroes in the making, and in doing so, to change the world—not because we are exceptional, but because we recognize that everyone, at their core, has the capacity to be extraordinary. Amen to that.

Peace and blessings!

Notes

Introduction

1. https://www.prisonpolicy.org/collateral.html.
2. https://www.prisonpolicy.org/reports/education.html.
3. https://acd.od.nih.gov/working-groups/wgd.html.
4. https://diversity.nih.gov/building-evidence/racial-disparities-nih-funding.
5. https://public.csr.nih.gov/AboutCSR/Evaluations#ECR_explanation.
6. https://extramural-diversity.nih.gov/diversity-matters/disadvantaged-backgrounds.
7. https://www.prisonpolicy.org/blog/2017/06/26/life_expectancy/.
8. https://www.fromprisoncellstophd.org/.
9. https://www.rand.org/pubs/research_reports/RR266.html.
10. https://www.prisonpolicy.org/reports/education.html.
11. Sheehy-Skeffington, J., & Rea, J. (2017). How Poverty Affects People's Decision-Making Processes. London: London School of Economics and Political Science. https://www.lse.ac.uk/business/consulting/assets/documents/how-poverty-affects-peoples-decision-making-processes.pdf.
12. The Color of Justice: Racial and Ethnic Disparity in State Prisons. October 13, 2021. https://www.sentencingproject.org/reports/the-color-of-justice-racial-and-ethnic-disparity-in-state-prisons-the-sentencing-project/.
13. Cohen, A., Vakharia, S. P., Netherland, J., & Frederique, K. (2022). How the war on drugs impacts social determinants of health beyond the criminal legal system. Annals of medicine, 54(1), 2024–2038. 10.1080/07853890.2022.2100926.

14. Galletta, E., Fagan, T. J., Shapiro, D., & Walker, L. E. (2021). Societal reentry of prison inmates with mental illness: obstacles, programs, and best practices. Journal of Correctional Health Care: The Official Journal of the National Commission on Correctional Health Care, 27(1), 58–65. 10.1089/jchc.19.04.0032.
15. How Mandatory Minimums Perpetuate Mass Incarceration and What to Do About It. February 14, 2024. https://www.sentencingproject.org/fact-sheet/how-mandatory-minimums-perpetuate-mass-incarceration-and-what-to-do-about-it/.
16. A better path forward for criminal justice: Reconsidering police in schools Ryan King and Marc Schindler. April 2021. https://www.brookings.edu/articles/a-better-path-forward-for-criminal-justice-reconsidering-police-in-schools/.
17. Brown, R. (2025). Freedom Isn't Free When You're Black and Poor. https://bailproject.org/learn/freedom-isnt-free-when-youre-black-and-poor/.
18. Hemez, P., Brent, J. J., & Mowen, T. J. (2020). Exploring the school-to-prison pipeline: how school suspensions influence incarceration during young adulthood. Youth Violence and Juvenile Justice, 18(3), 235–255. 10.1177/1541204019880945.
19. Private Prisons in the United States. By Kristen M. Budd, Ph.D. February 21, 2024 https://www.sentencingproject.org/reports/private-prisons-in-the-united-states/.
20. Harding, D. J., Wyse, J. J., Dobson, C., & Morenoff, J. D. (2014). Making ends meet after prison. Journal of Policy Analysis and Management: [The Journal of the Association for Public Policy Analysis and Management], 33(2), 440–470. 10.1002/pam.21741.

Chapter 2

1. Words From Prison—Did You Know...? https://www.aclu.org/other/words-prison-did-you-know.
2. Kajstura, A. & Sawyer, W. "Women's Mass Incarceration: The Whole Pie 2024," Prison Policy Initiative, March 5, 2024, https://www.prisonpolicy.org/reports/pie2024women.html.

Chapter 4

1. National Inventory of Collateral Consequences. "44,000 barriers to reentry." Bureau of Justice Statistics, https://niccc.nationalreentryresourcecenter.org/.

Chapter 6

1. https://www.youtube.com/@revolutionarytravelfamily/videos.

Chapter 8

1. Jury Partially Acquits Homicide Defendant. https://dcwitness.org/jjury-acquits-homicide-defendant-of-all-charges/.

Chapter 10

1. The European Forum for Restorative Justice (EFRJ), https://www.euforumrj.org/alternatives-detention.
2. The Abolition and Retention of Life Without Parole in Europe: A Comparative and Historical Perspective, https://brill.com/view/journals/eclr/4/3/article-p306_006.xml?language=en&.
3. How Some European Prisons Are Based on Dignity Instead of Dehumanization, https://www.brennancenter.org/our-work/analysis-opinion/how-some-european-prisons-are-based-dignity-instead-dehumanization.

Acknowledgments

As I reflect on the journey that led to the creation of this book, I am filled with gratitude for those who have supported me, both personally and professionally. First and foremost, I want to acknowledge my beautiful wife, Stephanie. Your unwavering strength, boundless love, and grounding presence have been my rock throughout this process. You have been my anchor, offering encouragement when I needed it most, and I am forever grateful for your support and belief in me. To my precious little girl, Ashlynn, our pumpkin pie, you light up my world with your laughter and joy. And to my son, William, you are the light that guides me, the future that I strive for, and the reminder of the beauty of life. I am blessed to call you both my children.

I would also like to express my heartfelt gratitude to the Prison to Professionals (P2P) community for embracing this vision and making it a reality. Your stories and resilience are the foundation of this book, and your strength serves as a constant reminder that transformative change is possible when we come together. A heartfelt thank-you to all the P2P Scholars who contributed their stories to this book. Your courage, resilience, and commitment to transformation are woven into every page, and your voices are a powerful testament to the strength of the human spirit. To the hundreds more who are not co-authors but who have walked this journey with us: your stories are just as transformative. They are stories that need to be told and heard, and they too shape the very fabric of this work. Thank you for being part of this community and for showing us what true strength looks like. Your contributions, whether written or lived, are invaluable.

Special Thanks

We would like to extend our deepest gratitude to Wiley for their unwavering support in helping us share the Prison to Professionals story. Your partnership has been instrumental in bringing this transformative narrative to life, and we are honored to have had the opportunity to work together. Thank you for believing in the power of these stories and for helping us amplify voices that deserve to be heard. Your commitment to this project is a testament to your dedication to meaningful change and the importance of lifting up marginalized communities.

Learn more about the Prison to Professionals community by visiting https://www.fromprisoncellstophd.org/.

About the Authors

Lead Author
Stanley Andrisse, MBA, PhD
Executive Director and Founder, Prison to Professionals (P2P)
Assistant Professor, Howard University College of Medicine

Baltimore, Maryland. Dr. Stanley Andrisse is a distinguished endocrinologist, educator, and social justice advocate dedicated to addressing systemic barriers within the criminal justice system and promoting higher education for formerly incarcerated individuals. As an assistant professor at Howard University College of Medicine, Dr. Andrisse combines his expertise in endocrinology with a passion for mentorship and transformative education. A formerly incarcerated person himself, Dr. Andrisse overcame significant personal and systemic challenges to earn his PhD in physiology from Saint Louis University and an MBA from Lindenwood University. His remarkable journey from incarceration to academia inspired him to establish Prisons to Professionals (P2P), a nonprofit organization that empowers justice-impacted individuals to achieve higher education and meaningful careers. Under his leadership, P2P has become a beacon of hope, helping countless individuals rewrite their life stories. Dr. Andrisse's academic research focuses on diabetes, insulin resistance, and the endocrine system, with a particular interest in how these issues intersect with public health in marginalized communities. His work has garnered numerous accolades, including appointments to prestigious committees and advisory boards aimed at fostering systemic change, such as the Lived Experience Advisory Committee for Maryland Governor Wes Moore's Task Force on Reentry Services. In addition to his academic and nonprofit work, Dr. Andrisse is a sought-after speaker and author, sharing his compelling story and insights on platforms ranging from national conferences to the White House, where he has spoken on health policy reform. Dr. Andrisse's unwavering commitment to justice, education, and public health continues to inspire and drive meaningful change in both the academic and broader social justice communities.

Contributing Authors
Kelsie L. Becklin, PhD (P2P Cohort 14, March 2020)

Minneapolis, Minnesota. Postdoctoral researcher and advocate for criminal justice reform, Dr. Kelsie Becklin is a dedicated postdoctoral researcher in the Webber Lab, where she continues her groundbreaking work on pediatric sarcoma models. Her research leverages induced pluripotent stem cells and genetic engineering to create innovative bottom-up models that reveal the early stages of cancer initiation and transformation. Through this work, Dr. Becklin aims to unlock new pathways for personalized therapeutic development, offering hope for more effective treatments for these devastating diseases. Her journey into the world of science is uniquely inspiring. Having navigated the challenges of the criminal legal system, her lived experiences have shaped her commitment to advancing both science and social justice. Following her presidential pardon, Dr. Becklin has emerged as a powerful advocate for criminal justice reform, using her platform to raise awareness about the transformative power of education and the potential for second chances. Outside of the lab, Dr. Becklin enjoys watching her son excel in sports, riding horses, and exploring the culinary scene in her city. Her story is a testament to resilience, the pursuit of knowledge, and the drive to make a meaningful impact both in science and in society.

William Freeman, BS (P2P Cohort 8, June 2019)

Baltimore, Maryland. William Freeman III is a powerful advocate for criminal justice reform and education in prison. After serving

20 years for murder, Freeman was released in 2018 and went on to earn his degree in sociology and anthropology from Goucher College through the Goucher Prison Education Partnership. Today, Freeman is a Bloomberg Fellow and a master's candidate at the Johns Hopkins School of Public Health. He works at the Education Trust, where he helps empower formerly incarcerated individuals and advocates for policy changes that close opportunity gaps for marginalized students. Through his involvement in the P2P Scholars Program, Freeman has further dedicated himself to breaking down barriers for those impacted by the criminal justice system, ensuring they have the tools and opportunities to transform their lives. His personal journey from incarceration to higher education illustrates the profound impact of education as a tool for personal growth and systemic change.

Lisa Guirsch-Webb, BS (P2P Cohort 35, December 2023)

Portland, Oregon. Lisa Guirsch-Webb's journey is one of resilience and transformation. After facing a tumultuous past, including a standoff with police and years of incarceration, she found strength through faith, education, and her relationship with co-author Rachel Guirsch-Webb. While in prison, Lisa Guirsch-Webb immersed herself in spiritual growth and education, even becoming a GED math teacher.

Her time in prison, especially in Oregon, was challenging, but it set the stage for a profound personal turnaround. Since her release, Lisa Guirsch-Webb has been dedicated to reentry and higher education initiatives. She joined AmeriCorps to help build Project Rebound at Portland State University (PSU) and became deeply involved in advocacy for justice-impacted individuals. Her passion for education was reignited after reading Dr. Stanley Andrisse's book, which inspired her to pursue higher academic goals. Now, Lisa Guirsch-Webb is an alumna of the Prison to Professionals Scholar Program, actively contributing to the mission of empowering formerly incarcerated individuals. She serves on various committees and boards, working tirelessly to improve reentry services and educational pathways for others. Lisa and Rachel, who defied the odds of maintaining a prison relationship, are now role models in their community, committed to supporting others on their journey of redemption and success.

Rachel Guirsch-Webb, BS (P2P Cohort 35, December 2023)

Portland, Oregon. Rachel Guirsch's life story is one of resilience, transformation, and the pursuit of education against all odds. Her journey began with a series of personal and legal challenges, including time spent in Coffee Creek Correctional Facility, where she grappled with the harsh realities of incarceration and the struggle to maintain her humanity. Despite the adversity, Rachel found purpose in working within the prison infirmary and supporting her peers, even amid the chaos of wildfire evacuations and the isolating effects of the COVID-19 pandemic. Following her release, Rachel embraced higher education as a beacon of hope, enrolling at Portland State University just days after her parole. Her commitment to personal growth led her to become a scholar with Prison to Professionals, where she connected with a community of like-minded individuals dedicated to breaking barriers and achieving academic excellence. Rachel's determination to turn her life around and inspire others serves as a powerful reminder that even after a fall, it is possible to rise, rebuild, and thrive.

Phillip A. Jones (P2P Cohort 23, October 2021)

Airway Heights Corrections Center, Washington State. Phillip A. Jones, Jr., is the founder and CEO of Phillip A Jones Consulting, LLC. Phillip was born and raised in the challenging environs of southwest Baltimore. Phillip's early life was deeply entangled with the stark realities of gang violence and poverty. A pivotal moment came at the age of 19 when a drug-related altercation led him to shoot another individual, who thankfully survived. This incident resulted in Jones receiving a daunting sentence of two life terms plus 20 years, marking the beginning of more than three decades of incarceration. However, Phillip's story does not end there; it transforms. In the crucible of prison, amid a landscape where hope is a rare commodity, Jones embarked on a journey of profound self-reinvention. Today, as the founder and CEO of Phillip A. Jones Consulting, LLC, he stands as a testament to the power of change, dedication, and hard work. Phillip has become a beacon of hope for many incarcerated and formerly incarcerated women and men. His dedication underscores an inspiring narrative of redemption, resilience, and the unwavering belief of second chances.

Brian L. Metcalf, EdD (P2P Cohort 28, January 2023)

Chicago, Illinois. An unapologetic advocate for the forgotten who centers human experience and relationships, Dr. Brian L. Metcalf has extensive experience in K-12 education both in traditional and charter school systems as well as nonprofit organizations. As a young teenager, Brian dreamed of becoming a teacher because he knew firsthand the power that schools possess to change the trajectory of children and communities. Dr. Metcalf spends time mentoring individuals impacted by laws designed to create caste systems. In his spare time, Dr. Metcalf enjoys culinary experiences and time with family and friends.

Tenaj Moody, MS (P2P Cohort 13, February 2020)

Washington, District of Columbia. Tenaj Moody is an internationally renowned educator and keynote speaker in domestic violence, sexual violence, criminal legal system, and mental health. She is the founder of Light To Life and two-time best-selling author. She is a licensed behavior specialist and has her master's degree in criminal justice with a certification in applied behavioral analysis. As an Afro-Latina millennial raised in North Philadelphia, who survived domestic violence, poverty, and having a parent who was incarcerated growing up; her experiences quickly taught her the power in owning her story and resilience. She has made it an obligation to share her story to impact, inspire, and uplift the often overshadowed voices through her social enterprise Light To Life, her research on women's health issues, and her best-selling book *Carry It with You.* Her accompanying personal testimonies rooted in these lived experiences have fostered an unwavering commitment to shift the narrative around violence prevention education and advocacy.

Tommy Moore, MBA, PhD (P2P Cohort 14, March 2020)

Omaha, Nebraska. Dr. Thomas Moore (aka Dr. Tommy) has a PhD in business administration (financial management) with more than 20 years of experience working in recovery and life coaching. After serving nine years and three months in the Florida Department of Corrections, he brings his lived experience and zeal for "withness" to the reentry workspace. Dr. Tommy shines when working with people ready to put effort into taking steps needed for positive and productive change. Through accountability, the focus on one's well-being, and SMART goals for healthy living, he has seen hundreds of lives changed. In his free time, Dr. Tommy enjoys weight lifting, swimming, deep-sea fishing, and spending time in nature. A fun fact about him is one leg is slighter shorter than the other, so that swagger in his walk? He's turned a so-called "defect" into a strength. Dr. Tommy is currently teaching at the Reception and Treatment Center in Lincoln, Nebraska.

Elhadji Ndiaye (P2P Cohort 25, April 2022)

Washington, District of Columbia. Elhadji Ndiaye is a student in the Howard University and Baltimore City Community College Bridges to Baccalaureate (B2B) program. An entrepreneur at heart, he helps manage his family business while also serving as the newly appointed CEO of his own venture, which he and his team plan to incorporate in 2025. Passionate about entrepreneurship, social and political sciences, and the arts, Ndiaye channels his experiences into creating meaningful intellectual property and uplifting both professional and aspiring creatives. His journey has been shaped by adversity—having navigated the justice system from birth, from shelters to federal penitentiaries. Despite a challenging past, he has emerged determined to redefine his future. Now at 25, he is committed to making the next chapter of his life his best yet. Ndiaye's story is one of perseverance, self-discovery, and an unwavering belief in the power of second chances. Through his work, he aims to inspire others to reclaim their futures, just as he has reclaimed his own.

Judith Negron, MS (P2P Cohort 21, June 2021)

Miami, Florida. Judith Negron is a criminal justice reform advocate with a master's degree in mental health counseling and more than 30 years of experience as an educator, mentor, and counselor to a diverse population in the mental health sector. As a formerly incarcerated individual, she has dedicated her freedom to advocate for those who have been directly and indirectly impacted by the criminal legal system, assisting in the pathways to fairness and equality in their future. Founder and CEO of The Freedom Glow, LLC, her mission is to empower others and guide them upon their reentry process; and her passion is to give a voice to those left behind, particularly to the children of the incarcerated, who are often the silent victims of these circumstances. Judith is a Prison to Professionals scholar and mentor, Speaker's Bureau member, The LOHM Pathways for Equity Fellow and Epic Ambassador for Florida, and Dream.Org Justice Advocacy cohort graduate; she also sits on the board of directors for Evolution Reentry, a support group for systems-impacted individuals.

Oswald Newbold II, BS (P2P Cohort 28, January 2023)

West Palm Beach, Florida. Oswald Newbold's journey from facing early life challenges to becoming a global advocate for justice and conflict resolution is a testament to resilience and transformation. Born to teenage parents and navigating the economic struggles of the 1970s, Oswald experienced early exposure to racial prejudice and disengagement from education. Despite these hurdles, his life took a dramatic turn at 19 when legal troubles led to a life sentence, prompting a profound decision to fight for change and embrace personal growth. Through mentorship, education, and sheer determination, Oswald re-entered society, overcoming systemic stigmas to secure a government job, rise to management, and complete his college degree. His involvement with Prison to Professionals helped him channel his experiences into inspiring others and fostering healing. Today, Oswald makes a positive impact through global advocacy work, criminal justice reform, and conflict mediation, continuously striving to empower communities and promote equity on a global scale.

Desiree Riley, BS (P2P Cohort 34, September 2023)

Philadelphia, Pennsylvania. Desiree "Dezi Speaks" Riley is the mother of five wonderful humans, a social entrepreneur, a visionary, and an alumna of Ohio State University with a focus on helping to shape this world into a better place for everyone. She is a recent graduate of the Reform Advocacy Institute and a participant in the thirty-fourth cohort of Prison to Professionals. Dezi also earned first place in the 2024 Ford Philanthropy Fellowship powered by Watson Institute. Her most recent publication includes *Felony to Freedom: Journey to Liberating an Institutionalized Mind*. Dezi spends most of her time traveling, homeschooling, and serving her community through the MasterMind Cooperative, a 501c3 personal development nonprofit she founded post-incarceration.

Mancy Thompson (P2P Cohort 3, June 2018)

Hanover, Pennsylvania. Mancy Thompson's journey from the streets of Baltimore to the battlefields of Beirut and eventually back home is a testament to resilience and redemption. Growing up in a challenging environment, Thompson sought escape through the Marine Corps, where he faced not only the horrors of war but also the lingering effects of racial tension and personal trauma. His life took a tragic turn when a post-service incident led to a 23.5-year incarceration. Despite the hardships, Mancy emerged determined to rebuild his life. After his release, he connected with Dr. Stanley Andrisse and joined the P2P Scholars Program, which reignited his purpose. By 2021, he became Prison to Professionals' program director, using his experiences to inspire and guide others. Today, Thompson is dedicated to helping justice-impacted individuals find their path, proving that second chances can lead to profound transformations.

Index

A
Abuse, evidence (documentation), 29
Adverse childhood experiences (ACEs), 53
Adversity, facing, 103
Advocacy, 57–59, 141
    change catalyst, 60–61
    global advocacy, 16–17
    second-change advocacy, voice (usage), 74–75
    story, 19
Aha moment, 112
Asghedom, Ermias Joseph, 126
Awareness, absence (impact), 157

B
Bank robbery, attempt, 109–110
Barriers, breaking, 57–58
Battlefield, impact, 191
Becklin, Kelsie, 196
    Andrisse meeting, 101–102
    photo, 117
Behavior, recklessness, 70
Belonging
    performance, 174–175
    sense, 160
Bible, reading, 90
Bridges, building, 57–58
Bridges to Baccalaureate program, 119–120

Briggs, Carol, 39
Business, control, 95

C
Call to action, 171
Career choices, changes, 57
Change
    catalyst, 60–61, 71–73
    path, 195
Childhood
    chaos, 137–138
    struggles, 68–69
Choices, consequences, 84
Coffee Creek Correctional Facility, 142–143, 145
    chaos, wildfires (impact), 143
Collective voices, usage, 59–60
Community, power/sense, 58–60
Comparison traps, 92
Compassion fatigue, 33
Complicity, impact, 43
Convictions, 10
Corrupt individuals, avoidance, 96
COVID-19 pandemic, 144
    love, discovery, 139–140
Criminal justice system, reform (need), 157–158, 162
Criminal record, disqualifications, 55
Culture shock, 69

D

Daily rituals, creation, 95
DeVos, Betsy, 175
Domestic violence
  epidemic, 29
  resources, 32
Dream, attempt, 94
Drugs, misuse, 105–110
Du Bois, W.E.B., 180

E

EBN Firm, 128
Education
  change catalyst, 71–73
  importance, 145, 164
  path, selection/creation, 157, 181
  power, 67, 145
  pursuit, 101–102
  survival, importance, 42–43
  value, understanding, 6–7
Education Trust National, 170
Ego checks, conducting, 95
Electroconvulsive shock, therapy, usage/impact, 106
Emergency numbers (safety document), 30–31
Empathy, increase (need), 161
Employment, difficulties, 74–75
Entrepreneurship, 73–75
Equal Justice Initiative, 197–198
Ethos, guidance, 156
Exit 2 Excellence (Jones), 163

F

Failure, success (relationship), 91
Faith, 69–71, 90, 137
Fear, impact, 126
Felony to Freedom (Riley), 82

Financial trauma, cycle (breaking), 85–86
Forcefulness, importance, 96–97
Foundation, building (Goucher College attendance), 175–176
Freedom, 140, 169
  double-edged sword, 172–174
  personal freedom, initiation, 90–91
  pursuit, 93
Freeman, William, 197
  Andrisse, meeting, 169–170
  belonging, performance, 174–175
  call to action, 179–181
  foundation, building (Goucher College attendance), 175–176
  freedom, double-edged sword, 172–174
  individual/collective identity, bridging, 178–179
  Johns Hopkins, transitioning, 177–178
  photos, 182–185
  tribe, finding, 176–177
Friend, assistance, 32–33
From Prison Cells to PhD (Andrisse), 74, 127, 140
Future
  focus, 128
  prison, feeling, 127
  reclamation, 36
Future vision, 93–97

G

Garvey, Marcus (teachings), 154, 156
Goucher College, attendance, 172–177
Goucher Prison Education Partnership (GPEP), 176
Grief, impact, 104–105
Guilt, untangling, 47

Guirsch-Webb, Lisa
    ashes, escape, 135–141
    childhood, chaos, 137–138
    devastation/hope, 137
    freedom/future fight, 140
    love (COVID era), 139–140
    mission (finding), P2P (usage), 140–141
    prisons, 138–139
    redemption, journey, 135–141
    suicide mission, 135–136
Guirsch-Webb, Lisa/Rachel, 196–197
    Andrisse, meeting, 133–134, 140, 141
    contraband gifts, 147
    mother, meeting, 148
    photos, 149–150
    wedding gift, 148
Guirsch-Webb, Rachel
    Coffee Creek prison, 142–143
    education, importance, 145
    love (hopeless place location), 142, 144
    P2P, joining, 146
    pandemic/isolation, 144
    reentry, 145
    wildfire evacuation, 143

H

Healed wounds, strength, 3
Healing, 88–89
    initiation, 189
    process, continuousness, 97
Hero withing, 198–199
Hinn, Benny, 69
Home confinement, breaking, 128
"House Made of Ashes, A" (essay), 119, 121–127

I

Ideas, intimidation (absence), 95
Identification (safety document), 30
Identity/dignity, sense, 154
Imposter syndrome, battling, 55–57, 61
Incarceration
    business classes, 71
    destructiveness, 142
    economic hardship, relation, 119
    exit/building, 86–87
    experience/reality, 45, 161
    inevitability, perception, 121
    issues, awareness, 58
    journey, 53–54, 178–179
    physical barriers, overcoming, 81
    poverty, intersection, 120
    reform, need, 164–165
    romantic relationships, ban, 139–140
    structural issues, impact, 197
Individual/collective identity, bridging, 178–179
Informational resources, 29
Injustice, 5
    systemic injustice, 195
    system, redemption (struggle), 187–189
Inner circle, building, 89–90
Institutionalized mind, liberation (journey), 79
Insufficiency/unworthiness, feelings, 72
Intelligence, stereotype (challenge), 7
Internal demons, battle, 55–56
Interstitial time, 104
Introspection, impact, 165

J

Jessup Correctional Institution, 156
Job opportunities, 14–15
    denial, 54–55

Johns Hopkins
    funding, 20
    mentors/allies, importance, 178
    transitioning, 177–178
Jones, Phillip Alvin
    Andrisse, meeting, 153–154
    evolution, 153
    photo, 168
Joseph Anointing: From Prison to Prosperity (McCray, et al.), 13
Justice
    narrative, rewriting, 3
    system, reform (need), 157–158
Justice Fellows Policy Program, application, 170
Justice-impacted students, expectations/investment, 174, 178–179, 181
JustLeadership USA, Leading with Conviction (LwC) Cohort, 16

K
King, Jr., Martin Luther, 122
Knowledge, quest, 155–157, 159

L
Ladies of Hope Ministries, 59, 61
Legal paperwork (safety document), 30
Legal system
    involvement, 43–46
    problems, 45
Libra-Life International, impact, 16–17
Life (lives)
    hardships, 4–5
    mistake, 44
    misunderstanding, 25–26
    pause, 104
    potential, 124, 127–128
    rebuilding/reclaiming, 70–71, 93
    regret, 166

sentencing, 10–13, 155–161, 167
    totality, metric (understanding), 21–22
    transformation, P2P (usage), 198–199
    violence/resilience, 189
Light to Life, mission/impact, 26–27, 32
Love
    COVID era, 139–140
    display, importance, 95
    hopeless place (location), 142, 144

M
Malcolm X, teachings, 154, 156
Mandela, Nelson, 81
Maryland Correctional Adjustment Center, 155–156
Maryland Correctional Institution, 173
Medication
    abuse, 105–107
    drug treatment, 106
Mentorship, 12–13, 16, 67, 115–117
Metcalf, Brian, 196
    Andrisse meeting, 35–36, 45
    background/early life, 37–40
    educational journey, 40–43
    legal system, involvement, 43–46
    personal growth/redemption, 46–47
    transformation/legacy, 47–49
Mission (finding), P2P (usage), 140–141
Mistakes, attention, 126–127
Money, saving, 29
Moody, Tenaj, 195–196
    Andrisse meeting, 19–20
    informational resources, 29
    photo, 34
Moore, Tommy Everette, 196
    Andrisse meeting, 67
    childhood struggles/early trauma, 68–69

224
Index

education, change catalyst, 71–73
entrepreneurship, 73–75
faith/resilience, 69–71
hope, message, 76
photos, 76, 77
relationship, restoration, 75–76
Mother, contradictions, 37
Murder, acquittal, 129

N

Narrative(s), 161
reading, 156
reflection, 171–172
rewriting, 20
shared narrative, 165
transformation, 170
National Association of Reentry Professionals, Inc. (service), 16
National Conference on Higher Education in Prison (NCHEP), 140–141
Ndiaye, Elhadji Babacar, 196
Andrisse, meeting, 119–120
ashes, escape, 127–129
"House Made of Ashes, A" (essay), 119, 121–127
photo/illustration, 130
Negron, Judith, 196
advocacy, change catalyst, 60–61
Andrisse meeting, 51–52
bridge building/barrier breaking, 57–58
community power, 58–60
emotional toll, 55–57
impostor syndrome, battling, 55–57
incarceration, journey, 53–54
opportunities, creation, 58–60
photos, 63, 64

reentry
reinvention, equivalence, 51, 62–63
reentry, challenges, 54–55
self-doubt, battling, 55–57
silent barriers, 54–55
stereotype, breaking, 53–54
voice, discovery, 57–58
Newbold II, Oswald, 195
Andrisse meeting, 3–4
photo, 17

O

Opportunities
creation, 58–60
pathways, creation, 181

P

Parents, relationship (improvement), 75
Patience
lessons, 85
need, 72
Perry, Tyler (internship opportunity), 128
Perseverance
journey, 79–80
success, 67, 72
Personal freedom, initiation, 90–91
Personal growth, 46–47, 87–88, 154–155
commitment, 81
Personal transformation, 195
Peters, Charles, 171, 175
Police, interaction, 107–109
Positive mindset, 85, 97
Poverty
criminalization, 80–81
facing/exposure, 21, 53
impact/weight, 3, 19, 79, 120, 133–134
presence, 119
realities, 153, 161

Power, regaining, 26
Practice, perfection (relationship), 94
Prejudice, term (understanding), 6
Presidential clemency, 53–54
Priority One Coaching, Counseling & Consulting, 75
Prisons, 138–139
    dehumanization, 154
    lessons, 85
    mentorship, 12–13
    schooling/studies, 10–14, 139–140, 171–172
    sentences, bias, 188–189
        United States Sentencing Commission study, 11
    women, existence (discussion), 24–25
Prison to Professionals (P2P)
    founding, 74
    frustration, sharing, 176–177
    healing, initiation, 189
    involvement/joining, 80–81, 146, 159–160, 169, 178
    mentorship, 115–117
    resources/support/opportunities, 51–52
    revelation/lifeline, 45, 46, 102
    Scholar Program, 141, 198
    scholars, empowerment, 198–199
    training, 15–16
    usage, 140–141, 192, 198–199
Procrastination, avoidance, 96
Product/service/trade, focus, 94
Project Phoenix, 86
Project Rebound, 140
Purpose
    educator journey, 35
    finding, 13, 47
    focus, 124
    narrative, rewriting, 3

R

Rebuilding, challenge, 47
Recidivism, 16, 101, 164
Redemption, 46–47, 193
    educator journey, 35
    journey, 135–141
    struggle, 187–189
Reentry, 52, 145
    challenges, 54–55
    journey, support, 58–59
    reinvention, equivalence, 51, 62–63
    work, transition, 15
Reintegration
    challenge, 71–72
    impacts, 60
    success, 162
Rejection
    impact, 54–56, 72
    leveraging, 176–177
Relationships, restoration, 75–76
Resilience, 69–71, 154, 159, 189
    celebration/embracing, 81, 89–90
    educator journey, 35
    lessons, 85
    story, 19, 193
    success, 67, 72
Respect, importance, 39, 154
Restorative justice, principles (impact), 158
Restorative practices, introduction, 42
Riley, Desiree, 196
    Andrisse meeting, 79–81
    encouragement/advice, 91–92
    financial trauma, cycle (breaking), 85–86
    healing, 88–89
    incarceration, exit/rebuilding, 86–87
    lessons, learning, 84–85
    ongoing journey/vision, 93–97

personal growth/transformation, 87–88
photo, 82
progress, 90–91
resilience, embracing, 89–90
self-reflection, 88–89
success, advice, 92–93
turning point, 83–84
Risk 2 Resilience (Jones), 163

S

Safe spaces, creation, 26–27
Safety
   documents, requirements, 30–31
   plan, preparation (process), 29
   word, creation, 29
Schools
   administrator role, 40–43
   reentry, 112–117
   transformation, 39–43
School/teachers, prejudices, 5–8
School-to-prison pipeline, 11, 163–164
School Without Walls, 123
Second Chance Pell (SCP) Experimental Sites Initiative, 176
Self-betterment, desire, 159
Self-discipline, importance, 91
Self-discovery, process, 87
Self-doubt, battling, 55–57
Self-empowerment, 154
Self-healing, 93
Self-perception, 166
Self-reflection, 88–89
Sentencing
   arbitrariness, 53
   harshness, 80
Sexual abuse, 22, 69
Shakur, Assata (teachings), 154, 156
Short-term memory, loss, 106

Siegel, Beanie, 83
Skill set
   impact, 62
   questioning, 56
Small operational changes (SOCs), implementation, 96
Society, reentry, 52
Sound therapy, practice, 96
Sovereignty, initiation, 90–91
Spaces, creation, 58–59
Stereotype
   breaking, 53–54
   rejection, 159
Stevenson, Bryan, 197–198
Story, sharing, 95
Structural racism, impact, 195
Success
   advice, 92–93
   meaning, 49
Suicide, consideration, 70
Support system, need, 86
Survival coping mechanisms, 69
Systemic barriers/roadblocks, 19, 54, 101
   dismantling, 60–61
   voice, usage, 57–58
Systemic injustice, 195–196
   fight, 4
Systemic oppression, impact, 170
Systemic racism, impact, 187

T

Teaching, passion, 38–43
The MasterMind Cooperative (TMC), 80–82, 86, 94
Thompson, Mancy, 197
   Andrisse, meeting, 187–189, 192
   battlefield impact, 191
   beginnings, 190

Thompson, Mancy (*continued*)
  Marine Corps, involvement, 190–191
  murder (incident), 191
  photo, 193
  prison, 191–192
  second chance, P2P (usage), 192
Tolliver, Linda, 136
Transformation, 87–88, 154
  lives (transformation), P2P (usage), 198–199
  personal transformation, 82, 195
Trauma, 68–69, 107–108
  stress, 88
Tribe, finding, 176–177
Trust, requirement, 93
Truth
  living, 180
  speaking, 28

U

Uniqueness, recognition, 95
United States of America vs. Elhadji B. Ndiaye, 122
University, attendance/issues, 9–10
Unlock Higher Education, 59, 61
US Army, joining, 8

V

Values, reassessment/realignment, 161
Vicarious trauma, 33
Victimization, 22–27, 196
Vision, 92, 97
Vulnerability, 155
  punishment, 133–134
  requirement, 93

W

Wall: Behind and Beyond, The (podcast), 162–163
War on Drugs, prison sentences, 188–189
Washington Corrections Center for Women (WCCW), 137
Williamson, Raquan (death), 123
Women
  dignity, fight, 24
  incarceration (Prison Policy report), 23
  problems, 125
  societal/historical disadvantages, 25
  strength/resilience, celebration, 27–28
  victimization, viewpoint, 22–23, 27
  Virginia Slave Laws, impact, 23–24
Women, world cruelty, 22–33

Y

Youth, mentoring, 16